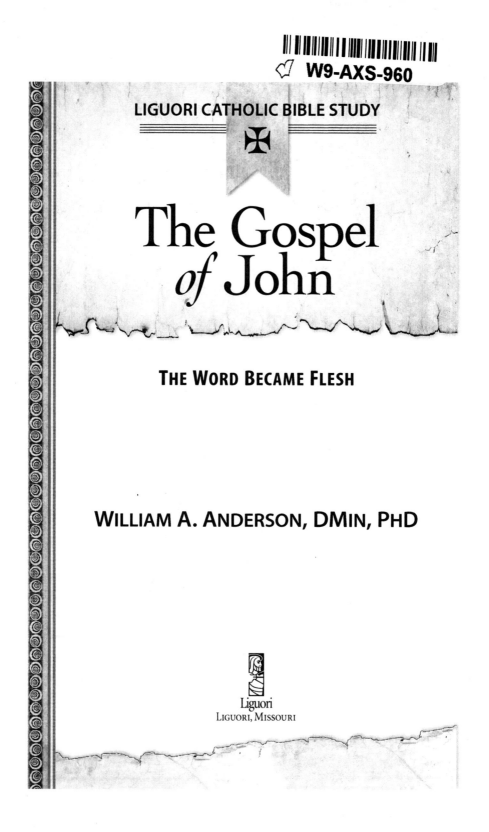

W9-AXS-960

LIGUORI CATHOLIC BIBLE STUDY

The Gospel
of John

THE WORD BECAME FLESH

WILLIAM A. ANDERSON, DMIN, PHD

Liguori
LIGUORI, MISSOURI

Imprimi Potest: Harry Grile, CSsR, Provincial
Denver Province, The Redemptorists

Printed with Ecclesiastical Permission and Approved for Private or Instructional Use
Nihil Obstat: Rev. Msgr. Kevin Michael Quirk, JCD, JV
            Censor Librorum
Imprimatur: + Michael J. Bransfield
            Bishop of Wheeling-Charleston [West Virginia]
            January 6, 2012

Published by Liguori Publications
Liguori, Missouri 63057

To order, call 800-325-9521
www.liguori.org

Library of Congress Cataloging-in-Publication Data

Anderson, William Angor, 1937-
    The Gospel of John : the word became flesh / William A. Anderson.—1st ed.
        p. cm.
1. Bible. N.T. John—Textbooks. I. Title.
    BS2616.A53 2012
    226.5'07—dc23
                                                              2012020228
p ISBN 978-0-7648-2123-3
e ISBN 978-0-7648-6725-5

Liguori Publications, a nonprofit corporation, is an apostolate of the Redemptorists. To learn more about the Redemptorists, visit Redemptorists.com.

Printed in the United States of America
16 15 14 13 12 / 5 4 3 2 1
First Edition

Contents

NOTE: The length of each Bible section varies. Group leaders should combine sections as needed to fit the number of sessions in their program.

Dedication

This series is lovingly dedicated to the memory of my parents, Kathleen and Angor Anderson, in gratitude for all they shared with all who knew them, especially my siblings and me.

Acknowledgments

Bible studies and reflections such as those in this current text depend on the help of others who read the manuscript and make suggestions. I am especially indebted to Sister Anne Francis Bartus, CSJ, DMin, whose vast experience and knowledge were very helpful in bringing this series to its final form.

Introduction to
Liguori Catholic Bible Study

READING THE BIBLE can be daunting. It's a complex book, and many a person of goodwill has tried to read the Bible and ended up putting it down in utter confusion. It helps to have a companion, and *Liguori Catholic Bible Study* is a solid one. Over the course of this series, you'll learn about biblical messages, themes, personalities, and events and understand how the books of the Bible rose out of the need to address new situations.

Across the centuries, people of faith have asked, "Where is God in this moment?" Millions of Catholics look to the Bible for encouragement in their journey of faith. Wisdom teaches us not to undertake Bible study alone, disconnected from the Church that was given Scripture to share and treasure. When used as a source of prayer and thoughtful reflection, the Bible comes alive.

Your choice of a Bible-study program should be dictated by what you want to get out of it. One goal of *Liguori Catholic Bible Study* is to give readers greater familiarity with the Bible's structure, themes, personalities, and message. But that's not enough. This program will also teach you to use Scripture in your prayer. God's message is as compelling and urgent today as ever, but we get only part of the message when it's memorized and stuck in our heads. It's meant for the entire person—physical, emotional, and spiritual.

We're baptized into life with Christ, and we're called to live more fully with Christ today as we practice the values of justice, peace, forgiveness, and community. God's new covenant was written on the hearts of the people of Israel; we, their spiritual descendants, are loved that intimately by God today. *Liguori Catholic Bible Study* will draw you closer to God, in whose image and likeness we are fashioned.

Group and Individual Study

The *Liguori Catholic Bible Study* series is intended for group and individual study and prayer. This series gives you the tools to start a study group. Gathering two or three people in a home or announcing the meeting of a Bible-study group in a parish or community can bring surprising results. Each lesson in this series contains a section to help groups study, reflect, pray, and share biblical reflections. Each lesson except the first also has a second section for individual study.

Many people who want to learn more about the Bible don't know where to begin. This series gives them a place to start and helps them continue until they're familiar with all the books of the Bible.

Bible study can be a lifelong project, always enriching those who wish to be faithful to God's Word. When people complete a study of the whole Bible, they can begin again, making new discoveries with each new adventure into the Word of God.

Lectio Divina
(Sacred Reading)

BIBLE STUDY isn't just a matter of gaining intellectual knowledge of the Bible; it's also about gaining a greater understanding of God's love and concern for creation. The purpose of reading and knowing the Bible is to enrich our relationship with God. God loves us and gave us the Bible to illustrate that love. In an address before the Pontifical Biblical Commission on April 12, 2013, Pope Francis stressed, "the Church's life and mission are founded on the word of God which is the soul of theology and at the same time inspires the whole of Christian life."

The Meaning of *Lectio Divina*

Lectio divina is a Latin expression that means "divine or sacred reading." The process for *lectio divina* consists of Scripture readings, reflection, and prayer. Many clergy, religious, and laity use *lectio divina* in their daily spiritual reading to develop a closer and more loving relationship with God. Learning about Scripture has as its purpose the living of its message, which demands a period of reflection on the Scripture passages.

Prayer and *Lectio Divina*

Prayer is a necessary element for the practice of *lectio divina*. The entire process of reading and reflecting is a prayer. It's not merely an intellectual pursuit; it's also a spiritual one. Page 18 includes an Opening Prayer for gathering one's thoughts before moving on to the passages in each section. This prayer may be used privately or in a group. For those who use the book for daily spiritual reading, the prayer for each section may be repeated each day. Some may wish to keep a journal of each day's meditation.

How to Use This Bible-Study Companion

THE BIBLE, along with the commentaries and reflections found in this study, will help participants become familiar with the Scripture texts and lead them to reflect more deeply on the texts' message. At the end of this study, participants will have a firm grasp of the Gospel of John and realize how that Gospel offers spiritual nourishment. This study is not only an intellectual adventure, it's also a spiritual one. The reflections lead participants into their own journey with the Scripture readings.

Context

When each author wrote his gospel, he didn't simply link random stories about Jesus—he placed them in a context that often stressed a message. To help readers learn about each passage in relation to those around it, each lesson begins with an overview that puts the Scripture passages into context.

Part 1: Group Study

To give participants a comprehensive study of the Gospel of John, the book is divided into eight lessons. Lesson 1 is group study only; Lessons 2 through 8 are divided into Part 1, group study, and Part 2, individual study. For example, Lesson 2 covers passages from John 2:1 through 4:54. The study group reads and discusses only John 2:1 through 3:21 (Part 1). Participants privately read and reflect on John 3:22 through 4:54 (Part 2).

Group study may or may not include *lectio divina*. With *lectio divina*, the group meets for ninety minutes using the first format on page 16. Without *lectio divina*, the group meets for one hour using the second format on page 16, and participants are urged to privately read the *lectio divina* section at the end of Part 1. It contains additional reflections on the Scripture passages studied during the group session that will take participants even further into the passages.

Part 2: Individual Study

The gospel passages not covered in Part 1 are divided into three to six shorter components, one to be studied each day. Participants who don't belong to a study group can use the lessons for private sacred reading. They may choose to reflect on one Scripture passage per day, making it possible for a clearer understanding of the Scripture passages used in their *lectio divina* (sacred reading).

A PROCESS FOR SACRED READING

Liguori Publications has designed this study to be user friendly and manageable. However, group dynamics and leaders vary. We're not trying to keep the Holy Spirit from working in your midst, thus we suggest you decide beforehand which format works best for your group. If you have limited time, you could study the Bible as a group and save prayer and reflection for personal time.

However, if your group wishes to digest and feast on sacred Scripture through both prayer and study, we recommend you spend closer to ninety minutes each week by gathering to study and pray with Scripture. *Lectio divina* (see page 11) is an ancient contemplative prayer form that moves readers from the head to the heart in meeting the Lord. We strongly suggest using this prayer form whether in individual or group study.

GROUP-STUDY FORMATS

1. Bible Study and *lectio divina*

About ninety minutes of group study

- ✠ Gathering and opening prayer (3 to 5 minutes)
- ✠ Scripture passage read aloud (5 minutes)
- ✠ Silently review the commentary and prepare to discuss it with the group (3 to 5 minutes)
- ✠ Discuss the Scripture passage along with the commentary and reflection (30 minutes)
- ✠ Scripture passage read aloud a second time, followed by quiet time for meditation and contemplation (5 minutes)
- ✠ Spend some time in prayer with the selected passage. Group participants will slowly read the Scripture passage a third time in silence, listening for the voice of God as they read (10 to 20 minutes)
- ✠ Shared reflection (10 to 15 minutes)
- ✠ Closing prayer (3 to 5 minutes)

To become acquainted with lectio divina, *see page 11.*

2. Bible Study

About one hour of group study

- ✠ Gathering and opening prayer (3 to 5 minutes)
- ✠ Scripture passage read aloud (5 minutes)
- ✠ Silently review the commentary and prepare to discuss it with the group (3 to 5 minutes)
- ✠ Discuss the Scripture passage along with the commentary and reflections (40 minutes)
- ✠ Closing prayer (3 to 5 minutes)

Notes to the Leader

- ✠ Bring a copy of the *New American Bible*, revised edition.
- ✠ Plan which sections will be covered each week of your Bible study.
- ✠ Read the material in advance of each session.
- ✠ Establish written ground rules. (Example: We won't keep you longer than ninety minutes; don't dominate the sharing by arguing or debating.)
- ✠ Meet in an appropriate and welcoming gathering space (church building, meeting room, house).
- ✠ Provide name tags and perhaps use a brief icebreaker for the first meeting; ask participants to introduce themselves.
- ✠ Mark the Scripture passage(s) that will be read during the session.
- ✠ Decide how you would like the Scripture to be read aloud (whether by one or multiple readers).
- ✠ Use a clock or watch.
- ✠ Provide extra Bibles (or copies of the Scripture passages) for participants who don't bring their Bible.
- ✠ Ask participants to read "Introduction: The Gospel of John" (page 19) before the first session.
- ✠ Tell participants which passages to study and urge them to read the passages and commentaries before the meeting.
- ✠ If you opt to use the *lectio divina* format, familiarize yourself with the prayer form ahead of time.

Notes to Participants

- ✠ Bring a copy of the *New American Bible,* revised edition.
- ✠ Read "Introduction: The Gospel of John" (page 19) before the first session.
- ✠ Read the Scripture passages and commentary before each session.
- ✠ Be prepared to share and listen respectfully. (This is not a time to debate beliefs or argue.)

Opening Prayer

Leader:　　O God, come to my assistance,

Response:　O Lord, make haste to help me.

Leader:　　Glory be to the Father, and to the Son, and to the Holy Spirit...

Response:　...as it was in the beginning, is now, and ever shall be, world without end. Amen.

Leader:　　Christ is the vine, and we are the branches. As branches linked to Jesus, the vine, we are called to recognize that the Scriptures are always being fulfilled in our lives. It is the living Word of God living on in us. Come Holy Spirit, fill the hearts of your faithful, and kindle in us the fire of your divine wisdom, knowledge, and love.

Response:　Open our minds and hearts as we study your great love for us as shown in the Bible.

Reader:　　(Open your Bible to the assigned Scripture(s) and read in a paced, deliberate manner. Pause for one minute, listening for that word, phrase, or image that you may use in your *lectio divina* practice.)

Closing Prayer

Leader:　　Let us pray as Jesus taught us.

Response:　Our Father...

Leader:　　Lord, inspire us with your Spirit as we study your Word in the Bible. Be with us this day and every day as we strive to know you and serve you and to love as you love. We believe that through your goodness and love, the Spirit of the Lord is truly upon us. Allow the words of the Bible, your Word, to capture us and inspire us to live as you live and to love as you love.

Response:　Amen.

Leader:　　May the divine assistance remain always with us.

Response:　In the name of the Father, and of the Son, and of the Holy Spirit. Amen.

The Gospel of John

Read this overview before the first session.

One Sunday morning, a man drove up to the curb outside a church building to pick up his wife after a celebration of the eucharistic liturgy. He decided to test the pastor, who was standing outside talking to people as they left. The man stepped out of his car and approached the pastor. As his wife stood by, embarrassed by her husband's bold challenge, the man pointed out that the people leaving worship were good, holy people who believed in God and already knew about God's dealings with them. The pastor agreed.

The man asked, "Why do we have to keep reading the Scriptures week after week? These people already know Jesus. What more can they learn? I come to pray, not to listen to something I already know. Why should I come each week to hear something over and over?"

The pastor said that the Scriptures and his homily speak about God's love and care for all people. The Scriptures are read during the liturgy, and the Church allows him as an ordained priest to enjoy the privilege of preaching about the readings to strengthen the faith of those in the assembly. Through the readings and his homily, the hope is that those worshiping can continue to show their love for God through their manner of life.

Pointing to the man's wife, the pastor asked whether she knew the man loves her.

The man looked at his wife, smiled, and answered, "Of course she does. I tell her I love her every day when I leave for work, and many times I tell her what she means to me."

The pastor asked, "Why? She already knows it. Does she have to hear it again?"

At first, the disciples continued to live their Jewish faith after the resurrection of Jesus, believing that Jesus was the Messiah, the Son of God. However, within a few decades after the resurrection of Jesus, the synagogue leaders began to realize that many of the Jews were converting to faith in Christ. At this astonishing development, they became indignant and angry with the Jewish Christians and expelled them from synagogue worship. It was becoming apparent that those who accepted Jesus as the Messiah were becoming noticeably different from those who did not believe that Jesus was the Christ. In 70, when the Temple was destroyed, the synagogue became the central place of worship for Judaism, and Christian Jews found themselves rejected by the strict Jewish culture. In many areas, they were ostracized and persecuted, leading the Jewish Christians to establish their own community.

In the midst of this persecution, an evangelist collected the traditions of the community and interpreted them for the Jewish Christians who were cut off from Judaism. Thus, the important messages found in the Gospel of John began to develop even further. The interpretations and development of the gospel traditions provided the foundation that the newly formed community needed for its existence outside the Jewish synagogue community. With the community's expulsion from synagogue worship, the members began to identify themselves as a Christian body independent from Judaism. Other followers of Jesus who were not affiliated with mainline Judaism became identified with the Johannine community as well, including gentiles from outside of Palestine. This led to some internal conflicts concerning the interpretation of the original Gospel of John, resulting in a series of changes that were brought together by a final editor.

Who Is John?

As it is with all the gospel writers, it is difficult to identify the author of the Gospel of John, especially when we examine the Johannine community. The composition of the gospel seems to have endured a number of transitions and changes. Tradition points to the Apostle John, the son of Zebedee and the brother of James, as the author. This traditional belief, although largely unchallenged through the centuries, was not widely accepted, even in ancient times. Saint Irenaeus, an early Christian writer, claimed at the end of the second century that John the Apostle was the author of this gospel, stating that he also penned the three letters of John and the Book of Revelation, an untrue statement, according to biblical scholars. After investigating the literary style and internal evidence in the texts, very few commentators agree that the same author wrote all these books. However, they do think it likely that the gospel writer also wrote some of the Letters of John in the New Testament.

The gospel speaks of "the beloved disciple" as the one who recorded these events (21:20–24). This disciple appears throughout the text, including chapter twenty-one, which is stylistically different from the rest of the gospel. According to scholars, this chapter was not written by the same author as the rest of John, posing a curious question about the identity of the "beloved disciple." In chapter 21, we read that Peter asked Jesus what would happen to the disciple whom Jesus loved, and Jesus states that he wants him to remain until he comes (21:20–22). Two verses later, we read: "It is this disciple who testifies to these things and has written them, and we know that his testimony is true" (21:24). Although chapter 21 has always been included in this gospel, it was clearly written by another author.

Some commentators believe the beloved disciple is often presented as one aligned in John's Gospel with Peter, even when he is not identified as the beloved disciple. For example, at the Last Supper, the one whom Jesus loved was reclining next to Jesus when Jesus announced that one of them would betray him. Peter signals the beloved disciple to discover the identity of that person (13:21–26). When Jesus is dying on the cross, he sees his mother and the disciple whom he loves, and he says, "Woman, behold your son," and looking at his disciple, he says, "Behold, your mother," but Jesus does not address the disciple as John. At the time of Jesus' resurrection, Mary of Magdala ran to announce the news to Simon Peter and "the other disciple whom Jesus loved" (20:3).

In other parts of the gospel, Peter is with "another disciple," whom commentators believe to be the beloved disciple. During the passion, when Peter comes into the courtyard with "another disciple," they are able to enter since the "other disciple" is known to the high priest. This incident hints that the "other disciple" was a Jewish follower of Jesus who may have lived in Jerusalem.

The author of the Second and Third Letters of John, which bear a strong resemblance to the Gospel of John, calls himself "the presbyter." Many attempts have been made to identify the author of the Gospel of John, but no conclusive evidence points to a specific author. The common opinion of scholars is that the author is an anonymous writer who gathered together and recorded the traditions developed within the Johannine community.

Date and Place

Most commentators place the writing of the gospel around the end of the first century, between the years 90 and 100. The author has some knowledge of the Gospel of Mark and, perhaps, of the Gospel of Luke. He shows familiarity with the destruction of Jerusalem, and his major issue is with the Jewish leaders who have cast all Christians out of the synagogues. The antagonism for the Jewish leaders is so great that the author no longer makes distinctions between the religious leaders of the Jews and the Jewish people. His gospel depicts an open conflict between Christians and Jews.

Fragments of the Gospel of John, dating from the early second century, have been found in Egypt. In order for the gospel to reach Egypt at this early date, it must have been written no later than the turn of the century; that is, no later than the year 100. Evidence points to the fact that it was written after the last of the synoptic Gospels, yet earlier than the first part of the second century. This leads to the speculation that the Gospel of John was written between 90 and 100.

The earliest tradition presumes that the Gospel of John was written at Ephesus, although some scholars claim it was written in Antioch or Alexandria. Most commentators find no reason to disagree with the earliest tradition, because the book could have reached Egypt (where the fragments were found) from Ephesus as easily as from any other main city of the Roman Empire.

The author writes with simple, common Greek terms, using words and images familiar to both his Hellenistic audience and those familiar with the Hebrew Scriptures. And the gospel is largely made up of discourses, with only a small amount of narrative material.

The Image of Christ in John's Gospel

John presents an image of Jesus the Christ in what scholars refer to as "High Christology," meaning that this gospel begins with the pre-existence of Jesus and stresses the divinity of Jesus throughout. In contrast, the Gospel of Mark, the earliest gospel written, begins with the baptism of Jesus by John the Baptist, and the Gospels of Matthew and Luke, written about fifteen to twenty years after Mark, begin before the birth of Jesus. The Gospel of John, the last gospel written, however, opens with Jesus' pre-existence: "In the beginning was the Word, and the Word was with God, and the Word was God" (1:1).

John presents Jesus as the divine Son of God who comes from God in heaven, enters our creation, and ascends to God again when his mission is complete. Throughout the gospel, John reveals a strong image of a divine Jesus who is thoroughly in control. John calls him the "Word" who existed with the Father from all eternity and through whom and with whom the Father created the world. In his very person, Jesus reveals God to those who see and understand him. In John's Gospel, although the Word becomes flesh, he retains all the powers of his divinity as the Son of God and speaks of himself as one with the Father.

The Gospel of Signs

In the synoptic Gospels, we read that faith must be present for Jesus to perform miracles. But John believes that the signs and wonders performed by Jesus lead to faith, and that Jesus' miracles point beyond themselves, bringing clarity to the message that Christ preaches. The Book of Signs consists of seven miracles or signs that lead people to faith in Jesus; though they might encounter a miracle or sign, they are invited to see more deeply—beyond the miracle. Some witnesses do not respond to these signs with faith, while others are able to encounter them with the eyes and ears of faith. John praises those who do not need signs in order to become believers.

life and the place of true worship, and, from a distance, heals the son of an official of the synagogue.

In Chapters 5 through 10, John portrays Jesus in conflict with those who misunderstand the meaning of the Sabbath. Jesus teaches about the Sabbath and performs healing actions on this special day of rest. He asserts his relationship to God, feeds the crowd in the desert, walks on water, and gives a discourse on the bread of life. Jesus uses the occasion of the feast of Tabernacles to present significant teachings about himself and the need for faith in him. Jesus ends his public ministry, and the passion story begins.

In Chapters 11 and 12, the cross begins to become a dominant theme. Jesus raises Lazarus from the dead, the leaders of the people react by deciding to have Jesus put to death, and Jesus is anointed in symbolic preparation for his burial. Jesus enters Jerusalem to shouts of praise, and he teaches the Greeks (the foreigners) who come to question him. The Book of Signs ends with a discourse on the message of the cross.

In Chapters 13 through 17, Jesus celebrates the Last Supper with his disciples, telling them that he will leave them for a time but will return. Jesus gives a long discourse concerning those who keep faith in him. The passage ends as Jesus prays for the Church.

In Chapters 18 through 20, John tells us about Judas' betrayal, Jesus' trial, Peter's denial, and the events surrounding the passion, death, and resurrection of Jesus.

Chapter 21, the text that most commentators believe did not originally belong to the first twenty chapters, pulls together some loose ends. In this chapter, we find Jesus appearing to his disciples in Galilee by the Sea of Tiberias, where he prepared fish and ate with the disciples. Also, here Christ forgave Peter and called him to a special mission within the Church.

Note About Terms Used in John's Gospel

When reading the Gospel of John, we must realize that John is speaking from the viewpoint of his own era, and he uses the expressions of his own time. Consider the following:

"Jews" in place of religious leaders: John will often speak of the Jews challenging Jesus instead of referring to the religious leaders, such as the Pharisees, the scribes, or the Sadducees, who are actually the ones who challenge Jesus. The use of the term "Jews" in place of the Jewish leadership has its roots in a deep struggle that existed between the Johannine community and the Jewish leadership. The community began to identify all the Jewish people with its leadership when some of the Jewish people joined the leaders in casting the converts to Christ out of the synagogues. In conclusion, we must recognize that although the author of the gospel uses the term "Jews" as being in conflict with Jesus, we should not read these accusations as referring to all the Jewish people of Jesus' day. Jesus himself was a devout Jew who "went according to his custom into the synagogue on the sabbath day" (Luke 4:16).

"Father" for the first person of the Trinity: Although John realizes that God is spirit, which means that he is neither male nor female, he uses the expression of the patriarchal era to identify God as "Father." In a commentary, it becomes difficult to avoid the use of the term "Father." When we read Jesus' words that state, "The Father and I are one," the message of the distinction of persons would be lost if we were to have Jesus say, "God and I are one."

"And the Word Became Flesh"

John 1:1–51

In the beginning was the Word, and the Word was with God, and the Word was God. He was in the beginning with God. All things came to be through him, and without him nothing came to be (1:1–3).

Opening Prayer (SEE PAGE 18)

Context

John the Evangelist begins his gospel by speaking of the pre-existence of the Son of God, identified here as the Word became flesh. He also speaks of the mission of John the Baptist's testimony concerning Jesus, and the first disciples' decision to follow Christ.

The first eighteen verses of John's Gospel serve as a prologue. Just as the musical overture in a play prepares the audience for the themes it is about to hear, so John uses the Prologue to present dominant themes heard throughout the gospel. He portrays Jesus as the divine Son of God sent to the world by God the Father. The Son of God enters creation and is named Jesus, who performs miracles, teaches, suffers, dies and is raised. More than in the Gospels of Matthew, Mark, and Luke, John stresses the divinity of Jesus and portrays him as thoroughly in control. In this gospel, Jesus speaks of himself as one with God the Father.

GROUP STUDY (JOHN 1:1–51)

Read aloud John 1:1–51.

1:1–5 The Word of God

The opening words of the gospel are the same as those found in the opening of the Book of Genesis: "In the beginning..." (Genesis 1:1). Here, the beginning refers directly to an existence before the beginning of the world, that is, the eternal that existed before time, creation, etc.... John uses the term "Word," to write about the Son of God noting that the Word of God is eternal as God is eternal. This reference to the "Word" is unique to John's Gospel. It may have some philosophical foundations that influenced the author of the gospel. However, the author does not use the term "Word" in an abstract sense but rather refers to a person who is God. In this way, he is drawing on his Hebrew background rather than making use of a philosophical connotation of the term.

The use of the term "Word" recalls the image of Wisdom found in the Old Testament Book of Wisdom, presenting Wisdom as a person who was with God before the beginning of the world, sharing in God's glory, and who will come to earth to guide human beings (Wisdom 9:9–11). Just as this Old Testament author speaks of Wisdom as a person, so the author of the Gospel of John refers to the Word as a person.

"The Word was with God" shows a relationship of presence between the Word and God. In the Book of Proverbs, we read that Wisdom was in the presence of God before the creation of the world (Proverbs 8:22–30). John tells us that the Word was not only with God, but was God. Through these opening words, John tells us that the Son of God, whom he identifies as the Word, was one with God from all eternity. John reveals a unity and a distinction between the Father and the Word by stating that the Word was God and, at the same time, that the Word was "with" God. This is a theme that will be developed throughout the gospel. The theological statements of the hymn present an overture for the rest of the gospel and reveal Jesus as the Word made flesh.

The Word of God is always creative, as we discover in the opening lines of the Book of Genesis (1:3ff). In the story of creation, God generates life with the spoken word. When God speaks, something happens. For this reason, the author of the Gospel of John can say that the Word existed with God from the beginning, and that everything in creation came into being through the Word. The author stresses creation through the Word by adding that "without him nothing came to be" (1:3).

Throughout the gospel, John uses contrasts, as he does with the contrast between light and darkness. A major theme of the gospel is the conflict between light and darkness. From the beginning, in the Prologue, John tells us the successful outcome of the Word in creation. Through the Word, life came to the world, and "this life was the light of the human race" (1:4). This life came to the world as light in the darkness, that is, as the light of faith and love in the midst of a world darkened by the power of evil. It is not merely the physical world, but also the spiritual world of God's love and grace that come to us through the Word. The light continues to shine in the darkness, and the darkness has not "overcome it" (1:5).

1:6–9 Testimony of John the Baptist

The author interrupts the hymn to introduce John, known as the Baptist in the Gospels of Mark and Matthew, but referred to as John alone in this gospel. Thus, John (the Baptist) is portrayed here as one sent by God, just as Jesus was sent by God. The term "sent" becomes thematic as well in the Gospel of John, for Jesus later appears to his disciples and sends them forth with the words, "As the Father has sent me, so I send you" (20:21). Likewise, Jesus speaks of being sent by God when he declares, "No one can come to me unless the Father who sent me draws him" (6:44).

Again there is a comparison made between John the Baptist and Jesus, for like Jesus, the Baptist accepted God's will when he was sent to testify to the light—to testify to Jesus, the Word of God made flesh. In the early Church period, some of John's followers believed that he was truly the Messiah since Jesus sought baptism from him, but John resolutely declares that he is not the light, but that he was sent to testify to the true light. He testified that Jesus, the true light that enlightens everyone, was coming into the world, and that the darkness of sin would be overcome by the light of Christ.

1:10–14 The Word dwelt among us

After this brief introduction of John, the author returns to the hymn, reiterating that the world came into being through the Word. But many in the world, including Jesus' own people, would not accept him. In the synoptic Gospels, we read that the people of Jesus' hometown rejected him, and some of his relatives sought to take him home with them, believing that he had gone mad. The author of the Gospel of John states that those who did accept him would receive the power of becoming children of God because they believed in him. John speaks of those who believe "in his name," meaning belief in the person of the Word.

By the grace of God, this faith made them children of God. Some scholars believe that the author of the gospel is referring to those from Jesus' own nation who did not accept him, and to those from among the gentiles who did. In the Gospel of Matthew, Jesus states, "For whoever does the will of my heavenly Father is my brother, and sister, and mother" (Matthew 12:50). The author emphasizes that it was God's choice, not our own, to grant us the gift of faith.

Although the author of the gospel writes that the Word of God became flesh, that is, became human and joined our human family by dwelling among us, he makes no mention of the birth of Jesus as found in the Gospels of Matthew and Luke. Instead, he uses images from the Old Testament. In the story of the Exodus, God directed Moses to set up God's tent (dwelling place) among the Hebrews in the desert (Exodus 33:7ff). In the tent, Moses asked God to permit him to see God's glory, but God allowed Moses to see only God's back.

The author of John's Gospel teaches that we have seen the glory of God in the Son who was sent from the Father. At this point, this links the Word to Jesus, naming him the Son of God and connecting him to the Father. John tells us that Christ alone can reveal the Father to us. Although John will later write in his gospel that "God is Spirit" (4:24) and therefore neither male nor female, he refers to God as both Father and Son throughout his gospel, a common way of referring to the persons of God in his day.

1:15–18 The witness of John the Baptist

The witness of the Baptist continues as he himself proclaims Jesus as the one who ranks above him, because he existed before the Baptist. In this passage, the Baptist is witnessing to the existence of the Son before the world began. The preexistence of Jesus is again stressed, but this time it was also a message sent to the disciples of the Baptist in the early Church era that might have still believed the Baptist to be the Messiah.

The gospel continues by revealing that we all share in the fullness of the grace of the Word become human. John the Evangelist declares that God's Law in the Old Testament comes through a human mediator, Moses, while grace and truth come through Jesus Christ. The grace of the New Testament derives from that of the Old Testament, described by the author here as "grace in place of grace." This shows the superiority of the gift that comes to us through the Word made flesh.

When Moses entered the tent in the Exodus event, he asked God to allow him to see God's glory. God tells Moses that no one can look upon God and live (Exodus 33:7ff). John the Evangelist explains that no one before Jesus has seen God, no matter how important and holy that person may have been. It is Jesus, however, who always shares in the glory of God and reveals God to us. It is through word and action that Jesus Christ reveals God to us, another major theme in the Gospel of John. Therefore, to see and understand Jesus Christ is to see and understand God.

1:19–28 John the Baptist identifies himself

In John's Gospel, we encounter "signs." A sign introduces a deeper message about the person of Jesus by his death, resurrection, and ascension. Each sign must be studied in its context in order to discover the message within it. Most of the signs, although not all, are miracles. This gospel thus distinguishes between "works" of Jesus and "signs," for the miracles not depicted as "signs" are referred to as the "works" of Jesus.

The first testimony begins with John the Baptizer explaining who he is. He debates with some priests and Levites who were sent from Jerusalem by the Jews. As mentioned in the introduction, the author made no distinction between the Jews and the religious leaders, as at that time the Jewish leaders refused to allow Christians to enter the synagogues. The priests and Levites had the duty of protecting the faith of the Jewish nation, and they attempt to fulfill their duty by questioning the Baptist about his mission. The followers of John believed that he was the Messiah or Elijah or one of the prophets.

According to the prophet Malachi, Elijah was to come before the day of the Lord (Malachi 4:5). Although the Baptist denies that he is Elijah, Jesus identifies him as the prophet Elijah in the Gospel of Matthew (Matthew 11:14). The priests and Levites ask John whether he is the expected prophet, and John answers that he is not. In the Book of Deuteronomy, Moses tells the people that God will raise up a great prophet like himself (Deuteronomy 18:15). Many saw this prophet as a type of Messiah.

After John denied that he was the Messiah, Elijah, or the great prophet, the priests and Levites ask him to tell them who he is so they can bring an answer to those who sent them. Although they do not explicitly ask their real question, they are seeking to know what gives him authority to preach and baptize. The priests and Levites want an answer to bring back to those who sent them. John responds by quoting from the Old Testament prophet Isaiah (Isaiah 40:3). He declares that he is the voice of one crying out in the wilderness whose duty it is to prepare the way of the Lord. The quotation originally referred to the Israelite nation and the Exodus episode in the desert, but it is used by the gospel writers to identify John's mission in preparing for the coming of Christ. John, who is preparing the way for the coming of Christ, uses the prophet Isaiah's message to identify himself.

The Pharisees now ask the real question about John's authority. Because John does not claim to be the Messiah, Elijah, or the prophet, some Pharisees challenge him to justify his authority to baptize. John responds that he baptizes with water, but there is someone in their midst, one whom they do not recognize, and with greater authority. They do not recognize him because they refuse to accept him. As successful and powerful as John is, he declares that he is not worthy to untie the thong of the sandal of the one who is now present in the world.

In Jesus' day, it was the role of a slave to take off the master's sandals as he entered the house and to clean the dust from his feet. The Baptist does not see himself worthy of performing even this lowly task for one as great as Jesus. According to the author, this episode took place at Bethany, across the Jordan. This is not the Bethany mentioned as the home of Lazarus but another Bethany that is not easily identified today.

1:29–34 John the Baptist's testimony about Jesus

This passage begins with the words, "The next day...," mirroring the opening words found in the Book of Genesis ("In the beginning..."); thus proceeding to tell what happened during the first seven days of Jesus' public life. In this way, he continues to follow the structure of the Book of Genesis, where the world is created in seven days (Genesis 1—2:3). The Gospel of John presents a message about the new creation, beginning with the Word become flesh. The first of the seven days of the new creation is marked by the Baptist's confrontation with the Jewish leaders regarding himself in relation to Jesus: "I baptize with water; but there is one among you whom you do not recognize, the one who is coming after me, whose sandal strap I am not worthy to untie" (1:26–27).

On the second day, John the Baptist identifies Jesus as the "Lamb of God, who takes away the sin of the world" (1:29). Isaiah spoke of a suffering servant being led like a lamb to the slaughter for the guilt and sins of many (Isaiah 53:7–12). The evangelist uses this image of the Lamb of God to link these words of John with the lamb sacrificed at Passover. On the Jewish feast of Passover, a lamb is slain as a remembrance of the Passover event recorded in the Book of Exodus, but the sacrifice is not for the removal of sin as it is when the lamb is led to slaughter in the book of Isaiah. The Gospel of John centers on Jesus, the paschal victim, who was crucified on Passover and became the new and eternal Lamb of God.

The evangelist already communicated John the Baptist's testimony to Jesus as one who has existed for all eternity. He repeats these words here as he witnesses to his disciples about Jesus. He tells his disciples that he did not know him. In the Gospel of John, there is no mention of the family relationship between the Baptist and Jesus as found in the Gospel of Luke. John states that the reason he came baptizing with water was so Jesus might be made known to Israel. In the Gospel of John, the Baptizer does not baptize for the forgiveness of sin, but to inaugurate the revelation of the Lamb of God to Israel.

Although John did not recognize Jesus at first, Christ was revealed to him when the Spirit, appearing as a dove, came from heaven and rested upon Jesus. In the synoptic Gospels, the action of the Holy Spirit was portrayed as being witnessed by Jesus alone. In John's Gospel, the vision of the Holy Spirit coming upon Jesus becomes the sign that identifies Christ for the Baptizer. John received an earlier revelation, namely that the person upon whom the Spirit comes down is the one who will baptize with the Holy Spirit. The reader of John's Gospel will immediately recognize that the author is referring to the sacrament of baptism, which comes to us from Jesus, who baptizes with the Holy Spirit.

In the synoptic Gospels, a voice from heaven proclaims that Jesus is "my beloved Son, with whom I am well pleased" (Matthew 3:17). In John's Gospel, it is the Baptist who proclaims that Jesus Christ is the Son of God. In the Book of the prophet Isaiah, we read that the suffering servant is God's chosen one: "Here is my servant whom I uphold, my chosen one with whom I am pleased" (Isaiah 42:1). This witness by the Baptist links the Son of God with the Lamb of God.

1:35–51 Jesus gathers disciples

The next day (the third day), two of John's disciples are present with the Baptizer when he, for the second time, proclaims that Jesus is the Lamb of God. The two disciples become followers of Jesus. The Gospel of John is the only one to mention the fact that some of the disciples of Jesus were previously followers of the Baptizer. When Jesus turns and sees them following him, he asks them what they are seeking. The disciples address him as "Rabbi," or "Teacher," a term that reveals how the disciples of Jesus viewed him during his public life. The disciples ask Jesus where he is staying, which is their way of asking if they can become his followers. The evangelist mentions that the time is four in the afternoon, a sign that the day is coming to an end.

Andrew is identified as one of the disciples who approaches Jesus, while the other, although unnamed, has traditionally been identified as John, the son of Zebedee. Other commentators believe that this other unnamed disciple is the one who will later be identified as "the beloved disciple," whose name is unknown and not one of the Twelve. Another group of commentators speculate that the other disciple is Philip, because he and Andrew each invite others to become disciples with them. Andrew tells his brother Simon Peter about Jesus and brings him to Jesus.

When Jesus meets Simon, he identifies him as a son of John and changes his name to Peter "Cephas" (1:42). According to Jewish tradition, a name change signified a call to a specific mission in life. In changing Simon's name to Cephus, an Aramaic name which means Peter, Jesus indicates that Peter has a special mission to fulfill. Jesus now has at least three disciples, but the manner in which they come to Jesus is different from those found in the synoptic Gospels where Jesus chooses his disciples. However, in this gospel, the first three disciples of Jesus come to him.

Because the two disciples come to Jesus late in the afternoon, many commentators see it as the end of the day, implying a new day (the fourth) has begun when Jesus meets with Peter. If this is so, the "next day," when Jesus calls Philip to follow him, would be counted as the fifth day. Philip came from the same town as Andrew and Peter, a town named Bethsaida, which had a mixture of Jewish and Greek culture. This could account for the Greek names of Andrew and Philip. The other disciples became followers of Jesus, apparently by their own initiative in John's Gospel, but Philip is the only one Jesus directly invites to follow him.

Just as Andrew went to Peter to tell him about Christ, so Philip goes to Nathanael to invite him to become a disciple of Christ. Because the name Nathanael is found nowhere among the list of Twelve found in the synoptic Gospels (John does not give a list), some commentators have tried to identify him with one of the other apostles. Many believe that Nathanael and Bartholomew were the same person, but there is no evidence to support this assertion.

The Jews of Jesus' day believed that the Messiah would come from Bethlehem, the birthplace of David, and not from Nazareth. When Philip tells Nathanael about Jesus of Nazareth as the one whom Moses wrote about in the law and who is also written about in the prophets, Nathanael scornfully asks whether anything good can come from Nazareth. This response may also indicate some animosity between Nathanael's hometown and Nazareth. Philip invites Nathanael to "come and see" (1:47), an invitation similar to that used by Jesus to Andrew and the other disciple.

When Jesus meets Nathanael, he calls him a "true Israelite" (1:47), in whom there is no pretense, that is, a person worthy to be called one of God's Chosen People. When Jesus speaks of seeing Nathanael under a fig tree, Nathanael enthusiastically proclaims his faith in Jesus as the Son of God and the king of Israel. A fig tree is often used as a symbol of peace. Although Nathanael addresses Jesus as the Son of God in this passage, he may have been referring only to the title of Messiah. The author of the gospel has already revealed that Jesus Christ is truly the Son of God, but he shows throughout the gospel that this discovery comes only gradually to Jesus' disciples. Jesus asks Nathanael if he believes because he said he saw him under a fig tree. He tells Nathanael that he will witness much greater things, an allusion to the miracles and the death and resurrection of Jesus.

Jesus tells his disciples that they will see the heavens opened and "the angels of God ascending and descending upon the Son of Man" (1:51). He uses the expression, "Amen, amen" (1:51), a phrase meant to stress the statement that Jesus is about to speak. The words of Jesus should remind us of an event in the life of Jacob, who awoke one night to find messengers from heaven ascending and descending a ladder to heaven (Genesis 28:12–13). Jacob had a visitation from the Lord at that time that foreshadowed the coming of the Lord in the person of Jesus Christ. The evangelist uses the term Son of Man in this gospel to refer to Jesus Christ in the fullness of his glory as the messianic king.

Review Questions

1. Why does John begin his gospel with the opening words from the Book of Genesis? Compare and contrast Genesis 1 to John 1 and discuss the similarities and differences.

2. Who is the *Word became flesh* in the Prologue? Explain.

3. How does the author identify John the Baptist?

4. What does the author mean when he says that "the Word became flesh and made his dwelling among us" (1:14)?

5. What does the Baptist mean when he calls Jesus the "Lamb of God" (1:29)?

6. What is significant about the manner in which Andrew, Philip, Peter, and Nathanael become followers of Jesus?

Closing Prayer (SEE PAGE 18)

Pray the closing prayer at this time or after *lectio divina*.

Lectio Divina (SEE PAGE 11)

Relax your body and maintain a posture of prayer (back straight, eyes shut, feet flat on the floor). This exercise can take as long as you want, but in the context of this Bible study, ten to twenty minutes should be sufficient.

The meditations that follow are provided only to help group participants use this prayer form, but note that *lectio* is intended to bring one to a place of prayerful contemplation where the Word of God speaks to the hearer from his or her heart. See page 11 for further instruction.

1:1–5 The Word of God

The opening of John's Gospel begins with the astounding news that the Son of God, the Word who existed from all eternity, became flesh and dwelt among us. The Word was always with God, existing from and for all eternity. Thus, the Word became flesh marks the beginning of the new creation. Christians believe there are three persons in one God and that the Word is the second person of the Trinity. The message of the new creation is that Jesus is God and is the Light of the World who gives life to the world. Darkness cannot overcome light, but light can overcome darkness. This is God, the second person of the Trinity, who brings life to the world and who will be the light of the world.

✠ *What can I learn from this passage?*

1:6–9 Testimony of John the Baptist

The Scriptures often use the image of darkness to refer to sinfulness. Many of those who are living in the darkness of sin do not understand the value of living in the light. Jesus comes as the Light of the World, and John the Baptist witnesses to Christ, our light. Jesus came to shed new light upon the world, but those who lived without this light had no idea of their need for it. John the Baptist had the ministry of bringing those who lived in darkness to recognize the arrival of the Light of the World.

✠ *What can I learn from this passage?*

1:10–14 The Word dwelt among us

Despite the news that the world came into being through the power of the Word, there were people who rejected faith in the Word. These are the people who live in the darkness of sin and unbelief and who do not recognize the light. Those living by faith, however, accept Jesus and can recognize his glory as the Son of God. They are living in the light. For them, Jesus is the Son of God who became flesh to dwell among us. Faith has a great influence on the way people view the meaning of life.

✠ *What can I learn from this passage?*

1:15–18 The witness of John the Baptist

The Son of God is revealed to us at the beginning of John's Gospel like a great beam of light, able to pierce the darkness and reveal God's great love to us. Creation is God's plan, and God's great love involves us more deeply in that plan through the Word of God becoming human. The Son of God dwelling among us unveils how important we are to a loving God.

✠ *What can I learn from this passage?*

1:19–28 John the Baptist identifies himself

The authority of John the Baptist comes from God, and he baptizes with water, but there is someone coming who is greater than he. As Christians, we know who that "someone" is. John stated that he did not know the Lord until he saw the Spirit come down upon him. We now share in that gift of the Spirit, which enables us to have faith that Jesus is the Christ, the Son of God.

✠ *What can I learn from this passage?*

1:29–34 John the Baptist's testimony about Jesus

A central feast for Jews is Passover, when they sacrifice a lamb and share it at a ritual meal. This meal recalls the day God directed Moses to instruct the Israelites who were enslaved in Egypt to kill a lamb, paint its blood on their doorposts, and eat the lamb as people ready for flight. The angel of death killed all firstborn males in the households of those who did not have the blood marked on their doorposts. Jesus is here called the "Lamb of God," a hint that he will become the new sacrifice and new Passover. From the very beginning, Jesus is designated for this passion, death, resurrection, and ascension as the Lamb of God.

✠ *What lesson can I learn from this passage?*

1:35–51 Jesus gathers disciples

In the synoptic Gospels, Jesus chooses his disciples, but in John the disciples (with the exception of Philip) come to Jesus, who accepts them. The reality, however, is that Jesus already planted the desire in the hearts of Simon, Andrew, Philip, and Nathanael to become disciples. They were responding to God's grace granted to them. The reality is that we too have been called by the gift of grace and are responding to the invitation to follow the Lamb of God as the disciples did. The call to follow Jesus always begins with God calling us.

✠ *What can I learn from this passage?*

INDIVIDUAL STUDY

This lesson does not have an Individual Study component.

Jesus Gives Living Water

JOHN 2:1—4:54

Everyone who drinks this water will be thirsty again; but whoever drinks the water I shall give will never thirst; the water I shall give will become a spring of water welling up to eternal life (4:13–14).

Opening Prayer (SEE PAGE 18)

Context

Part 1: John 2:1—3:21 Mary, the Mother of Jesus, initiates Jesus' public ministry by requesting that Jesus change water into wine at the wedding feast at Cana. Jesus seems to object, but Mary ignores this and directs the servants to do what Jesus tells them. Following this event, Jesus casts the merchants and moneychangers out of the Temple. When challenged by the religious leaders, Jesus speaks of his body as a temple, saying that it will be raised up in three days. Jesus then teaches a lesson about baptism to Nicodemus and predicts his own death.

Part 2: John 3:22—4:54 John the Baptist supports Jesus' disciples who were baptizing a large number of people and teaching that power must come from God. After John the Baptist proclaims that he must decrease as Christ increases, Jesus declares that he is the one who comes from above. In this study, Christ promises living water to the woman at the well and returns to Cana where he heals a royal official's son.

PART 1: GROUP STUDY (JOHN 2:1—3:21)

Read aloud John 2:1—3:21.

2:1-12 The wedding at Cana

The wedding at Cana takes place "on the third day" (2:1). Nathanael came to Jesus on the fifth day, and the third day after Nathanael came to Jesus would be the seventh day. The reader should note that John does not say *three days later*, but *on the third day*, meaning that we would count the fifth day as the first day, the sixth as the second, and the seventh as the third. Just as there were seven days in the creation story, so these seven days mark the inauguration of the new messianic era. The *third day* is also reminiscent of the day when Jesus was raised from the dead. The third day in this passage shows that Jesus has moved into a new situation. His mission is about to begin.

Although no parables are found in John's Gospel, each episode and event in the gospel is filled with countless allegories. The first of these stories is the well-known narrative of the wedding feast at Cana. The theme of a wedding feast fits perfectly with the message the story wishes to convey. The coming of the messianic kingdom is often portrayed as a banquet or celebration. The wedding celebration is occasionally used to show that the Messiah is the true bridegroom at the banquet.

Jesus, his disciples, and his Mother are attending a wedding feast at Cana in Galilee. Jesus' mother has an important role in this story. When the wine runs out, Jesus' Mother speaks on behalf of the family and tells Jesus they have no wine. At the end of John's Gospel, Jesus will symbolically declare that Mary is the mother of all people when he says to Mary, "'Woman, behold, your son," and to the beloved disciple, "Behold, your mother" (19:26–27). The motherly instinct and concern shows itself at this point when the Mother of Jesus acts as though she is a mother concerned for all people.

During Jesus' era, a Jewish wedding feast could last for several days. It would be a terrible tragedy for the bride and groom to run out of wine before the celebration ended. When the wine runs out, the Mother of Jesus intervenes for the sake of the hosts. Nowhere in the gospel is she called Mary. When she tells Jesus that the hosts have no more wine, Jesus responds by addressing her as "Woman" (1:4), which was a title of honor and respect for a woman during Jesus' era, but hardly a title one used for one's own mother.

John makes it clear that Jesus hears his mother asking for a miracle, and Jesus' answer sounds harsh. He tells her that this cannot concern him, because his hour has not yet come. The "hour" ordinarily refers to Jesus' passion, death, resurrection, and ascension. Therefore, his first sign (miracle) would be the launching of his hour that would eventually lead to his passion, death, resurrection, and ascension. Unperturbed by his apparent rejection of her request, the Mother of Jesus directs the waiters to do whatever he tells them. Not only does the author of the gospel show that Jesus has full knowledge of his divinity, but he also shows that the Mother of Jesus is aware of Jesus' divine powers.

According to Jewish Law, those coming to a wedding feast had to perform certain ritual washings before taking part in the meal. The hosts at the wedding provided stone jars ordinarily filled with water for this ritual washing. Jesus orders the waiters to fill the jars with water. Each jar held about twenty to thirty gallons. When the jars were filled, Jesus orders the waiters to draw out some of the water that had become wine and to take it to the chief steward. The steward comments on the quality of the wine, which is better than that served at the beginning of the banquet.

This little episode has many messages hidden within it. The water in the stone jars used in Judaism for ritual washing signifies the old covenant, and thus changing water into wine marks the beginning of a new covenant. Jesus, the true bridegroom at the messianic banquet, brings the new and finer covenant (the good wine). The old creation has run out, and the new creation begins with Jesus. God has saved the good wine until last, that is, until the coming of Jesus.

The prophet Amos spoke about the coming of the messianic kingdom as a time when the juices of the grapes will run down the mountains. It is a time when the true Israel will be rebuilt (Amos 9:13–14). In both the old and new creations, wine symbolizes blood. When Jesus tells his mother that his hour had not come, he is linking the new wine with the eucharistic sacrifice. The celebration of the Eucharist is properly a celebration in which

Christ offers his blood for us, but it also celebrates the total mystery of his Passover into glory. Through the first of his signs, Jesus shows that the messianic era has dawned, revealing his glory. Thus the disciples begin to believe in Jesus.

In a transitional verse to the next episode, John tells us that Jesus, his Mother, his relatives, and his disciples go to Capernaum, where they remain only a few days. In the synoptic Gospels, Jesus spends the first part of his public ministry in Capernaum, his home during his ministry.

2:13–25 Cleansing the Temple

Following the miracle at Cana, John presents the episode of Jesus' cleansing of the Temple. In the synoptic Gospels, the cleansing of the Temple, which occurs toward the end of Jesus' life, becomes one of the reasons the leaders of the Jewish people seek to put Jesus to death. The author of John's Gospel places the cleansing of the Temple right after the first sign performed by Jesus at Cana to show that Jesus continues to replace the old Law with the new. The Temple, the very center of Jewish worship, must also give way to Christ, who is the temple of the new covenant.

John the evangelist tells us that Jesus was in Jerusalem to celebrate the feast of Passover. The synoptic Gospels tell of only one visit to Jerusalem by Jesus, while John reports that Jesus celebrated three Passover feasts there. In this instance, the Gospel of John is most likely correct. Jesus, being a devout Jew, would naturally wish to celebrate the Passover in the Holy City when possible. As Jesus enters the Temple area, he becomes enraged at what he encounters and, making a whip of cords, he drives out those who were selling the oxen, sheep, and doves used for worship, knocking over their tables, spilling their coins, and driving the animals out of the Temple area.

In Jerusalem, it was customary for the people to exchange their Roman coins for Temple coins, since the Temple could not be contaminated with a foreign coin. Jesus rejects making the Temple into a marketplace. In the synoptic Gospels, Jesus gives as a reason for cleansing the Temple of the cheating taking place on the merchants' part, and he quotes from the prophet Jeremiah who declared that the house of the Lord had become a den of thieves (Jeremiah 7:11). Though the author makes no mention of the den of thieves, he portrays Jesus as enraged because the Temple of God has become a marketplace.

During Jesus' era, the leaders of the Jews often confronted him and tried to turn the people against him. Approximately seventy years after Jesus' resurrection, when John writes his gospel, he does not make a distinction between the Jewish leadership and the Jewish people. He views the rejection of Jesus as coming from all the Jews and not the Jewish leaders alone. When the Jews challenge Jesus, he responds to their challenge with a confusing answer. He tells them to "destroy this temple" (2:19), and he will raise it up in three days. The Jews are amazed at his answer, reminding him that the temple has been under construction for forty-six years. According to ancient records, the construction of the Temple began about 20 BC, placing Jesus in Jerusalem somewhere near the year AD 27, a fairly accurate date for Jesus' public ministry.

The author of the Gospel of John clarifies Jesus' statement for us by explaining that Jesus was talking about the temple of his body. When John writes his gospel, he is already aware that the Jewish Temple had been destroyed around the year 70. After the resurrection of Jesus, the disciples (and the author of this gospel) would realize that Jesus was speaking about his own resurrection from the dead as the temple to be raised up in three days. The old Temple has been destroyed, but the new temple, Jesus, continues to exist. Because the Jews used Jesus' words about the destruction of the Temple at his trial during the passion, many commentators believe that Jesus actually spoke these words.

Many people come to believe in Jesus because of the signs he is performing, but Jesus remains cautious, not trusting them because he knows that their faith is weak. John tells us that Jesus knew human nature well and knew how the human heart worked. He knew that these same people would turn against him during his passion. Although Jesus does not perform any miracles in this passage, the author of the gospel considers it to be another of Jesus' signs. It shows that Jesus is the Messiah, the one who has great zeal for his Father's house, and the one who acts with authority in the Temple. He casts out the old Law for the new. The Temple of the old Law will give way to the temple of his body, the temple of the New Covenant.

3:1–21 Nicodemus

John introduces Nicodemus, a Pharisee and a member of the Jewish San-hedrin. As a member of the leading Jewish body, he is a powerful leader who comes to Jesus at night, a sign that he wanted to keep his visit a secret. Nicodemus will appear twice more in the Gospel of John, first to defend Jesus against his accusers (7:50–52) and later to take part in the burial of Jesus (19:39). He shows respect for Jesus by addressing him as "Rabbi." Nicodemus has seen the signs that Jesus performed, and the signs bring him to his first steps of faith. He cannot yet be called a believer, but he acts as one who is pondering what he has seen.

Nicodemus remarks that he knows Jesus comes from God, since no one can perform the signs Jesus is performing unless God is with him. Jesus ignores Nicodemus' words of praise and tells him that no one can enter the kingdom of God unless he is born from above. Jesus stresses his statement with the usual words of emphasis: "Amen, Amen, I say to you" (3:5). The author of John's Gospel uses a common literary device in this debate between Jesus and Nicodemus. Jesus makes a statement, and Nicodemus asks a question, which is followed by another statement by Jesus and another question by Nicodemus.

Viewing birth from a purely physical viewpoint, Nicodemus asks how a person can be born again. He asks sarcastically if a person can enter a mother's womb to be reborn. Jesus makes it clear that he is not talking about physical birth. He tells Nicodemus that the baptism by water, given by John the Baptist, does not lead one into the kingdom of God; but a new birth in water and in the Spirit does. He makes his statement strongly emphatic by again using the words, "Amen, Amen I say to you" (3:11).

Jesus states that a person of flesh can only give birth to another in the flesh, but the Spirit can give birth to a new spirit in a person. Jesus is talking about a spiritual birth from above, and he tells Nicodemus that this message should not surprise him. Just as the wind blows according to its own whim and a person is able to hear it without knowing its origin, so the Spirit touches everyone in the same way. Those begotten of the Spirit cannot tell us any more about the action of the Spirit. Knowing the origin of the Spirit and how the Spirit works cannot be fully understood.

The author plays on words here, since the word for Spirit and the word for wind is the same in the Greek language.

Jesus' answer leads Nicodemus to ask another question for further clarification. He asks Jesus how this can happen, and Jesus, accepting Nicodemus' role as a teacher, chides him for not understanding what Jesus is saying. In this passage, the author of the gospel is speaking about baptism as a sacrament, and such a message would be far beyond anyone's comprehension during the life of Jesus. Much of this explanation comes from knowledge gained by the author and other followers of Jesus after Jesus' resurrection and ascension.

After Nicodemus asks this question, he disappears from the scene in John's Gospel, and the dialogue between Jesus and Nicodemus now becomes a discourse given by Jesus to a larger audience, most likely the readers of the gospel. The author of the gospel frequently uses this literary technique of having someone ask a question which becomes the foundation for a longer discourse meant for a larger audience. Jesus, again speaking with the emphatic expression *Amen, Amen*, speaks as one who knows what he is preaching because he has seen God, whereas the people—that is, the Jewish people who do not have faith in Jesus—do not accept his testimony.

Note that Jesus was originally speaking to Nicodemus when he addressed him as "you," but John now presents Jesus as moving from addressing Nicodemus alone to addressing "you people." If people do not believe Jesus when he speaks about things of the earth (perhaps a reference to the wind), then how will they believe him when he speaks about heavenly things? Jesus declares that he can speak of heavenly things because he, the Son of Man, has come down from heaven. The expression *Son of Man* is used here to refer to Jesus in glory. In John's Gospel, Jesus is totally conscious of his coming from the Father.

John next refers to an event in the Exodus experience of the people of Moses' time. When the people of the Exodus sinned in the desert, God punished them by sending a multitude of poisonous snakes. After many people died from serpent bites, God directed Moses to set a brass symbol of the serpent on a pole so that all who looked at it would be saved from death (Numbers 21:4–9). Jesus alludes to this as a sign pointing to himself (the Son of Man) as he is lifted up on the cross to bring eternal life to those who believe in him. Jesus' teaching shows that he is aware of his crucifixion when he is speaking.

God's love is so great that God sent his only Son in order that those who believe in the Son may have eternal life. The Son of God did not come to condemn the world, but to save the world. Jesus does not condemn those who do not accept his presence in the world; they condemn themselves. This condemnation comes because the light came into the world, but some chose the darkness of sin and their evil ways instead of the light. Lest they be exposed, those who practice evil avoid the light, while those who live in truth come into the light so that their works may be plainly perceived as done in God. The contrast of light and darkness found in the gospel harkens back to the first chapter of John's Gospel when he writes that "the light shines in the darkness and the darkness has not overcome it" (1:5).

Review Questions

1. What is the significance of Jesus' actions during the wedding at Cana?
2. Why does Jesus cleanse the Temple? Explain the significance of it in this gospel.
3. What is the central message of Jesus' conversation with Nicodemus? What role does Nicodemus play in John's Gospel?
4. What authority does the Son of God have to witness God's activity in the world?

Closing Prayer (SEE PAGE 18)

Pray the closing prayer now or after *lectio divina*.

Lectio Divina (SEE PAGE 11)

Relax your body and maintain a posture of prayer (back straight, eyes shut, feet flat on the floor). This exercise can take as long as you want, but in the context of this Bible study, 10 to 20 minutes should be sufficient.

The meditations that follow are provided only to help group participants use this prayer form, but note that *lectio* is intended to bring one to a place of prayerful contemplation where the Word of God speaks to the hearer from his or her heart. See page 11 for further instruction.

The wedding at Cana (2:1–12)

At the bidding of his mother, Jesus enters his hour, that is, his path toward his passion, death, resurrection, and ascension. When we pray in honor of Mary, we are praying through a loving mother who has an overwhelming concern for our welfare as she had for the hosts of the wedding feast of Cana. We pray that Mary will help us on our mission in life. She is Our Mother of Perpetual Help, always ready to intercede on our behalf. Mary speaks to us as she did to the servants: Do whatever he tells you. At Mary's bidding, we abide by Christ's will.

✠ *What can I learn from this passage?*

Cleansing the Temple (2:13–25)

The worship area where the action of Christ in the Eucharist takes place is a type of temple. Although the merchants in the gospel were on the outer rim of the temple, Jesus considered the whole temple to be a place for reverence. It is his "Father's house" (2:16). Jesus had a sense of the sacred and challenges us to test our own sense of the sacred during the eucharistic celebration and our reverence for the place where the community joins together to worship in the name of Jesus.

✠ *What can I learn from this passage?*

Nicodemus (3:1–21)

Jesus tells us of heavenly things. His heavenly message for us is that we must be born of water and the Holy Spirit to enter the kingdom of God. Christians are born again through water and the Spirit in the Sacrament of Baptism, bringing us into union with Jesus, the Light of the World. Those who choose the light perform good deeds so that their "works may be clearly seen as done in God" (3:21).

✠ *What can I learn from this passage?*

PART 2: INDIVIDUAL STUDY (JOHN 3:22—4:54)

Day 1: The Final Witness of John the Baptist (3:22-30)

The author interrupts Jesus' discourse to speak about the witness of John the Baptist. Although we will find in chapter four that Jesus did not baptize (only his disciples did), it seems from this present passage that Jesus was baptizing with his disciples. Since chapter four specifically notes that Jesus did not baptize, we can presume that this is true. However, perhaps this reference is intended to emphasize the importance of baptism for Christians and the role disciples played in baptizing members of Christ's body.

The disciples of John the Baptist complain to him about the baptism given by Jesus and his disciples. At the time, John was baptizing at Aenon near Salim because of the abundance of water there, a sight that most commentators are not able to identify. The author of the Gospel of John tells us that the Baptist had not yet been imprisoned. In the synoptic Gospels, Jesus begins his public mission when Herod imprisons John, but the Gospel of John makes no mention of the Baptist being in prison. The Baptist's disciples seem to be jealous of Jesus' success as they report to John that Jesus, about whom the Baptist was testifying, is now drawing crowds to himself and baptizing them. This jealousy reflects the controversy in the early Church between the followers of John who believed he was the Messiah and the followers of Jesus.

The Baptist tells his disciples that no one possesses this gift unless it comes from above. He reminds his followers that he himself declared that he was not the Messiah but that he was sent before him to witness to Jesus. The author of the gospel may have added this statement from the Baptist to emphasize again that John the Baptist is not the Messiah. The Baptist calls Jesus the bridegroom and himself the best man, the one who exults at the voice of the bridegroom. Now that Jesus has arrived and his mission has begun, the Baptist's joy has reached its fulfillment. The Baptist proclaims that Jesus "must increase; I must decrease" (3:30). The time has come for the Baptist to step aside, and it is noteworthy that these words are the last words uttered by John the Baptist in the Gospel of John.

Lectio Divina

Spend 8 to 10 minutes in silent contemplation of the following passage:

The disciples of the Baptist are apparently jealous of the success of Jesus' disciples. Jealousy can exist among holy people who sincerely strive to fulfill God's will. John has the perfect antidote to jealousy, a mental attitude that recognizes the importance of Christ increasing within us as we decrease. No one should use their devotion or religious knowledge to lord over others, rather it should serve to humbly help and inspire them. The ability to touch the heart of another with a spiritual blessing comes from God, not from human ingenuity.

✠ *What can I learn from this passage?*

_____

Day 2: The One Sent From Heaven (3:31–36)

Some Scripture scholars believe this passage should immediately follow verse 21 of this chapter, before the passage about John the Baptizer, since its current placement seems to indicate that John the Baptist is speaking. The lesson found in this passage, however, clearly comes from Jesus. The scholars believe the author of the gospel slipped the episode about John the Baptist into the middle of Jesus' discourse, perhaps to remind the readers that the Baptist previously spoke of Jesus as the one who will baptize with the Holy Spirit (1:33).

The author of the gospel continues to make use of contrasts. In this passage, he begins by contrasting what is above (heaven) with what is below (earth). The one who comes from heaven, namely Jesus, is above all, while the one who adheres to the world can speak only in a worldly way. Christ testifies to those things he has seen and heard, but no one "of earth" accepts his testimony. Even if some do not accept the testimony of Jesus, those who do accept it witness to the truth of Jesus' words and experience the abundance of the gifts that come from the Spirit. The Father loves the Son and has turned everything over to him. Those who disobey the Son will not have life, meaning eternal life with God. Faith in the Son leads to eternal life, while rejection of the Son leads to the destruction that comes from God's wrath. The image of the wrath of God appears often in the Old Testament, punishing for the sake of atonement, not for condemnation. Jesus did not come to bring condemnation, but he warns about God's wrath for the sake of saving those who are obstinate and refuse to follow the light of Christ.

Lectio Divina

Spend 8 to 10 minutes in silent contemplation of the following passage:

> Jesus is God become human, and so he has the words of eternal life. Believing in Jesus means that we believe with words and deeds, a faith that affects our whole life in all we do. True belief is living what we say we believe. We believe Jesus came from heaven with true knowledge of God and shares this knowledge with us. We illustrate our trust in Jesus' message by making it visible in our lives.

✠ *What can I learn from this passage?*

Day 3: The Samaritan Woman (4:1–42)

To avoid the Pharisees, Jesus must withdraw from Judea and journey back to Galilee with his disciples. The Pharisees are the religious leaders of the people who led a persecution against the followers of Jesus within Palestine after the destruction of the Temple in 70. In Jesus' day, the Pharisees who did not believe in Jesus would have resented his action of casting the merchants and moneychangers out of the Temple. Jesus would naturally attempt to avoid the Pharisees who were likely upset with Jesus' disciples baptizing more people than the disciples of John. His journey to avoid the Pharisees takes him through Samaria and leads to his encounter with the Samaritan woman at the well.

During Jesus' lifetime, the Jews and the Samaritans were open enemies. In the late eighth century before the coming of Christ, the Assyrians invaded the northern kingdom of Israel, marching off some of its inhabitants into exile and bringing other conquered people of other nations into Samaria to intermarry with the Israelites. The Jews of Jesus' day looked down on the Samaritans who practiced a form of faith that mixed many

Jewish traditions with other traditions brought in by the pagan inhabitants. In Jesus' era, the animosity between the Jews and the Samaritans
was so great that they were openly hostile to each other to the point that
some Jews felt that they were unclean if they even spoke to a Samaritan.

On his journey through Samaria, Jesus stops to rest by a well, known as
Jacob's Well, in a town called Sychar. The Book of Genesis does not specifically
mention Jacob's Well, but it does speak about Jacob buying a piece of land
on which he pitched his tent (Genesis 33:18–20). It was in this place that
Jacob set up an altar and invoked the God of Israel. Biblical scholars contend
that it was on this plot of land where Jacob's Well was constructed. It was
apparently widely used by the people of Samaria for their water supply.

Exhausted, Jesus rested at the well around noon, while his disciples
journeying with him went into town for some food. A woman comes to
draw water from the well. When Jesus asks her for water, she expresses
surprise that he, a Jew, would ask her, a Samaritan and a woman, for a
drink. The Jews at the time considered Samaritan women as unclean, so
the Jews were naturally forbidden to drink from any vessel handled by
a Samaritan woman. Jesus, as was his custom, followed the Mosaic Law,
but he rejected laws developed over time by Jewish authorities, laws that
he considered to be contrary to the laws prescribed by Moses. The attitude
about contact with the Samaritans as being unclean came from a later interpretation of the Law by religious leaders. The author of the gospel notes
the animosity existing between the Samaritans and the Jews.

The woman's surprised response provides Jesus an opportunity to teach
his message. He tells her that she would have asked him for living water
if she realized the gift of God and who was asking for a drink. As in the
dialogue between Nicodemus and Jesus, the author of the gospel uses the
same literary form: Jesus makes a statement and the Samaritan woman
follows with a question. The woman at first misunderstands Jesus, believing that he is speaking about the fresh, living water from the well. Jesus
actually is speaking about spiritual water, the life-giving and eternal gift
of the Spirit.

The woman addresses Jesus as Sir, which is a greeting akin to addressing a man with great respect. She asks Jesus how he expected to get water
from such a deep well without a bucket, and she immediately follows this

question with another, asking where Jesus expects to draw this water. John shows us that she is beginning to understand the implications of Jesus' use of "living water" when she chides Jesus and questions whether he claims to be greater than Jacob who gave the people this well and used it for himself and his family. Although there is no mention of Jacob's Well in the Old Testament, oral tradition held that Jacob used the well for his family and flocks while he lived in the area.

Jesus answers the woman's question, not by answering that he is greater, but by stating that his gift is far more lasting than what Jacob provided. Jacob gave them water, but anyone who drinks it will eventually become thirsty again. Jesus, however, promises spiritual water that will never leave anyone thirsty. It will be as a spring of life within a person, "welling up to eternal life" (4:14). The woman again shows that she misunderstands Jesus' message when she asks him for this water that will keep her from having to come and draw from the well again. Any water that would quench one's thirst once and for all would be a great gift.

After the woman asks Jesus for this living water that will quench her thirst once and for all, Jesus ignores her statement and tells her to go and bring her husband to him. When she answers that she has no husband, Jesus agrees with her, stating that she has had five husbands and that the man she is living with now is not her husband. His answer causes the woman to regard Jesus in a new light. She now considers him a prophet of Israel and questions him about a major dispute between the Samaritans and the Jews, namely, the proper place for worshiping God.

The Samaritans believed their ancestors worshiped God on the mountain where the meeting between Jesus and the woman was taking place, while the Jews believed that true worship took place in Jerusalem. The mountain was at Gerisim, a place on which the Samaritans erected a temple in the fourth century before Christ. In answer to the woman's question, Jesus presents a theme that is central to the Gospel of John, namely, that true worship will no longer depend on a place but on one's faith and spirit. True worship according to Jesus will be done in "Spirit and truth" (4:23) rather than in either Jerusalem or at Gerisim, the mountain. Jesus tells her that the hour is coming when this change will occur. By using the word "hour," Jesus again links his message with his death, resurrection, and ascension.

Because of his hour, people will worship in Spirit and in Truth. Since God is Spirit, this will be the true worship desired by the Father.

The woman responds to Jesus' words by stating that she believes the Messiah is coming. Jesus tells her that he is the Messiah, saying, "I am he." This recalls the words spoken by God when addressing Moses in the Old Testament, when God called himself "I AM" (Exodus 3:14). Although Jesus does not seem to be speaking directly of his divinity here, he does seem to be preparing the way for a later statement in which he will refer to himself as I AM.

When the disciples return, they wonder about Jesus speaking with the woman, but none of them dares to question him about it. The woman, leaving her water jar behind as a sign she will return, calls the townspeople to come and meet Jesus. She wonders whether he could really be the Messiah. The townspeople set out to meet him.

Meanwhile, when the disciples urge Jesus to eat, he tells them that he has food of which they know nothing. The disciples are speaking of the ordinary food, while Jesus is speaking of spiritual food that consists in doing the will of the one who sent him and in carrying out his mission. The disciples ask each other whether someone else has brought Jesus food, a question that enables Jesus to launch into another discourse.

Jesus tells them that his food is the fulfillment of his Father's will. He quotes from a well-known proverb of the day, stating that the harvest would come in four more months. This may be a reference to the time between the planting and the harvesting. Jesus invites the disciples to look to the Samaritans to find a harvest ready for reaping. The disciples did not plant, but people such as Jesus, the Samaritan woman, and others planted, and the disciples of Jesus share in the harvesting. This may be a reference to the many Samaritans who became believers after the ascension of Jesus. At the harvest time, those who sow and those who reap share joyfully in the harvest.

When the Samaritans finally come to Jesus, they beg him to stay with them, believing in him because of what the woman told them. Jesus stays with them two days. At the end of that time, they are able to profess their faith in Christ, not because of the woman's testimony but because they themselves have heard Jesus' words. Unlike the Jews, who reject Jesus, the Samaritans profess that he is the Savior of the world.

Lectio Divina

Spend 8 to 10 minutes in silent contemplation of the following passage:

The story of Jesus and the Samaritan woman at the well obviously points to the living waters of the sacrament of baptism. Just as Jesus breaks the ritual rules of his day concerning speaking to a woman and a Samaritan, he also breaks the limitations of worldly thinking. He is the living water who brings about a great change in our lives. Those who drink will never thirst again. Once we celebrate the sacrament of baptism, we have no need to be baptized again. We celebrate the gift of baptism, the gift of being called sons and daughters of God and rejoice in the blessings and graces that God pours forth upon us—living water welling up to eternal life.

✠ *What can I learn from this passage?*

Day 4: Second Sign at Cana (4:43–54)

After two days, Jesus leaves Samaria for Galilee. John the Evangelist recalls that Jesus testified that a prophet has no honor in his own country. We find these words of Jesus in Mark's Gospel (Mark 6:4) where the people of Nazareth reject Jesus. But it is difficult to know why the author of John's Gospel placed the reference at this point in his gospel. A possible explanation is that the Samaritans believed in Jesus because of his words, whereas the Galileans believed in him only because of his signs. The Galileans' faith was not as solid as that of the Samaritans. The people of Galilee welcome Jesus because they had seen all that he had done while in Jerusalem at the Passover feast.

Jesus goes to Cana, where he had performed his first miracle. A royal official, hearing in Capernaum that Jesus has returned, goes to him and begs him to come and heal his ill son. The story is similar to that of the centurion and his sick servant in the Gospels of Matthew and Luke (Matthew 8:5–13; Luke 7:1–10). Jesus responds with a rebuke for all the people who must see signs in order to believe. The royal official persists in his request, and Jesus sends him home with the assurance that his son will live.

The author of the gospel tells us that the man believes Jesus and starts his journey home. Unlike the people of Galilee, the royal official believes without seeing. The passage teaches that Jesus' word is powerful, even from a distance. The official's servants meet him with the news that his son is well, telling him the time of the cure: the exact hour Jesus pronounced that the boy would live. The author states that this was the second sign Jesus performed on his return to Galilee from Judea.

Lectio Divina

Spend 8 to 10 minutes in silent contemplation of the following passage:

Jesus answers our prayers, often in unseen ways. We do not have to see the answer to our prayer to believe that God is answering it in some manner. Faith tells us that God loves us, and God answers our prayers in a way that we may not see, but the Lord sees. Faith is trust in a loving God who heals as God sees fit.

✠ *What can I learn from this passage?*

Review Questions

1. Why does John the Baptist show joy at the success of the baptism performed by Jesus' disciples?

2. What is the meaning of the living water that Jesus offers the Samaritan woman by the well?

3. What is the message of the Samaritans who came to believe in Jesus? Why is it significant?

4. How did Jesus heal the royal officials' son and what does it teach us?

Jesus, the Bread of Life

JOHN 5:1—6:71

When the people saw the sign he had done, they said, "This is truly the Prophet, the one who is to come into the world" (6:14).

Opening Prayer (SEE PAGE 18)

Context

Part 1: John 5:1–47 Jesus encounters conflict on a Sabbath when he heals a man who had been ill for thirty-eight years. When the Jewish leaders confront Jesus about this healing, Jesus retorted that his Father (meaning God) is at work just as he is and claims that he is doing everything in accordance with the will of the Father. Just as the Father raises the dead and gives life, so the Son gives life, and those who do not honor the Son also fail to honor the Father. Jesus urges his listeners not to be astounded at his works, while challenging the unbelief of those who do not believe that he comes in the Father's name.

Part 2: John 6:1–71 Jesus feeds five thousand with five barley loaves and two fish, and when the fragments were collected after the people ate, twelve baskets were filled, leading the people to declare that Jesus is the prophet who is to come. Later that evening, after the disciples had departed by boat and were rowing against a strong headwind, Jesus comes to them walking on the water, a miraculous sign pointing to Jesus' divinity. After this, the bread of life discourse takes place.

PART 1: GROUP STUDY (JOHN 5:1–47)

Read aloud John 5:1-47.

5:1–18 Jesus cures on the Sabbath

Jesus arrives in Jerusalem for a Jewish feast, which is unnamed by the author. He encounters a man who had been sick for thirty-eight years and hoped to be cured by going into the waters of the Sheep Pool, an apparently miraculous pool that was near the Sheep Gate in Jerusalem. The waters of this pool would bubble up and presumably heal the one who entered it first. A later writer attributed this to God by claiming that an angel came and stirred up the water. This heavenly visitation is not mentioned in the older manuscripts of this gospel. When Jesus asks the man if he wishes to be healed, the man tells Jesus that he has no one to put him into the water when it is stirred up. Jesus directs the man to stand, pick up his mat, and walk. The man is immediately cured and does as Jesus orders.

The episode recalls the story of Jesus healing the paralytic in the Gospel of Mark (Mark 2:1–12). The significance of this story in John, however, is that Jesus not only performs a miracle on the Sabbath, but he also tells the man to carry his mat on the Sabbath, an act strictly forbidden by Jewish law. When the Jews see the man, they ask him why he is carrying his mat on the Sabbath, and he answers that the man who restored his health ordered him to do so. The man later discovers that Jesus was the one who healed him, and he tells this to the questioning Jews. The author gives no motive for the man to give Jesus' name to the Jews. Some believe that he did it because his faith was still weak, and he did not understand the sign performed by Jesus, while others believe the man was trying to lead the Jews to Jesus so they could learn from him.

The Jews begin to persecute Jesus because of his apparent disregard for the Sabbath. In this episode, Jesus provides the people with an even greater reason to seek to persecute and kill him. He claims that he has the right to work on the Sabbath because God works on the Sabbath. The Jewish people believed that God sustains the world throughout every moment, a belief that demanded God work on the Sabbath. Jesus calls God "my Father," which was seen as making himself equal to God. This was considered blasphemy by the Jews and was punishable by death.

5:19–30 The ministry of the Son

The discussion concerning Jesus' right to work on the Sabbath and his relationship to the Father leads to a discourse by Jesus explaining the Son's relationship to the Father. As a true reflection of the Father, the Son states he can do nothing by himself, but only what he sees the Father doing. The Father, in his love for the Son, allows the Son to know all. Those who see Jesus as the reflection of the Father will see even greater works in the future, an allusion to the signs and wonders that Jesus is yet to perform.

Just as the Father works on the Sabbath, raising the dead and giving life to the newborn, so the Son grants life to whomever he wishes. By working on the Sabbath, Jesus granted new life to the sick man who could not move into the saving waters. The Father, who is judge of all, grants to the Son his power to judge. They are so closely united that honor for the Son is honor for the Father, and disrespect for the Son is disrespect for the Father. The hour is coming when those who have faith in the Father will share in eternal life. The power of judging given to the Son does not mean that the Son sits on a throne, inviting the good to heaven and casting sinners into hell. It means that Christ is the one who sets up new norms for judgment. The whole of creation, the living as well as the dead, must face this judgment. Because Christ is so faithful to the will of the Father, he can never be accused of being dishonest in his judgment. The norms set up by Christ are the same as those willed by the Father.

5:31–47 The witnesses to Jesus

Jesus calls on those who can witness on his behalf, knowing that his listeners will not accept his own testimony. He knows that the Father will testify about him and that his testimony can be proven true. John the Baptist was sent as a witness to Jesus, not because Jesus himself needed it, but for the sake of those who listened to him. The Baptist gave them light that led to Christ, but this lasted only for a short time. John was meant to lead to the light, but, unlike Jesus, he was not the light.

Now Jesus calls on another witness, namely the works that the Father has given him to do. The Father bears witness to the Son, but because the people do not accept the One he has sent, they are not capable of accepting the witness of the Father. The Scriptures accepted by the people as the Word of God also bear witness to Christ. But the listeners are unwilling to grasp the fullness of life given through the Scriptures.

Jesus is not speaking this way for human glory but because he comes in the name of his Father. Yet the people refuse to accept him. Those who come in their own name, seeking human praise, receive high recognition from people. Jesus asks them, "How can you believe when you accept praise from one another and do not seek the praise that comes from the only God" (5:44)? Jesus states that he will not have to accuse them before the Father because Moses, who gave them the Law, will stand as their accuser. If they cannot accept the teachings of Moses, how can they expect to believe what Jesus has to teach them?

6:1–15 Jesus feeds five thousand men

The scene changes abruptly from Jerusalem (in the last chapter) to Galilee and the shore of Tiberias. Some believe that these abrupt location changes indicate that the chapters may not be in the order the author originally intended. Others believe that John the Evangelist simply chose to write his chapters with little regard for geographical precision.

The crowd continues to follow Jesus, not because of his message, but because of the signs he is performing. Jesus, significantly, goes up a mountain and takes the position of authority on the mountain by sitting down. Jesus' trip up the mountain may be a parallel to Moses going up the mountain to receive the Ten Commandments. Just as the old Law was revealed on a mountain, so the New Covenant would be revealed on a mountain. John tells us that the crowd numbered five thousand men. In the era in which Jesus lived, women and children, who were most likely present, were not ordinarily counted. We are told here that the Jewish feast of Passover was near, the second one to be mentioned in the Gospel of John. The link between the multiplication of the loaves and the Passover feast is also significant, because the Christians at the time of the writing of this gospel saw a link between the Jewish Passover and the celebration of the Eucharist, as we do today.

The author of the gospel tells us that Jesus knew what he was going to do when he asked Philip where they would get enough food to feed so many people. John continues to present Jesus as completely in control of the situation. Philip echoes the frustrations of Moses in the desert when he states the impossibility of feeding so many people. When Andrew explains that a young boy has five barley loaves, hardly enough for such a vast crowd, Jesus has the people recline. He takes the loaves, gives thanks, and distributes them to the people; and he does likewise with the two fish.

All the gospel writers include Jesus' multiplication of the loaves, but only the author of John's Gospel adds that Jesus "gave thanks." The word for this action in Greek is the source of the word we use for "Eucharist," meaning "to give thanks" (6:11). When the disciples gather up the fragments, they fill twelve baskets with the fragments from the five barley loaves, a number that represents the twelve apostles of the New Covenant. There is no mention of gathering the fish. The people again misunderstand the message behind the miracle and declare that Jesus is the prophet foretold by Moses (Deuteronomy 18:15). They seek to make him king, but Jesus withdraws from them "to the mountain alone" (6:15).

Review Questions

1. What issue is raised when Jesus cures the sick man at the Pool of Siloam?
2. When Jesus claims that he is one with the Father, what explanation does he give? Give some examples.
3. What witness does Jesus give for his ministry in the name of the Father?
4. How does the multiplication of the loaves signify the Eucharistic Celebration?

Closing Prayer (SEE PAGE 18)

Pray the closing prayer now or after *lectio divina*.

Lectio Divina (SEE PAGE 11)

Relax your body and maintain a posture of prayer (back straight, eyes shut, feet flat on the floor). This exercise can take as long as you want, but in the context of this Bible study, 10 to 20 minutes should be sufficient.

The meditations that follow are provided only to help group participants use this prayer form, but note that *lectio* is intended to bring one to a place of prayerful contemplation where the Word of God speaks to the hearer from his or her heart. See page 11 for further instruction.

Jesus cures on the Sabbath (5:1–18)

Just as Jesus took the initiative in healing the sick man on the Sabbath, Jesus will do the same in our lives. He inspires us to respond to his message and assist others. Every good deed we perform, we do so through God's inspiration. We may think that the special prayers we pray or the faith we live are a result of our own thinking, but all good things come from God.

✠ *What can I learn from this passage?*

The ministry of the Son (5:19–30)

Jesus is the visible image of the invisible God (see Colossians 1:15). The great revelation of Jesus is that he actually offers us a living image of God. As Jesus loves, God loves. As Jesus forgives, God forgives. The love and compassion of Jesus reveal the great love and compassion of God. Jesus says, "I do not seek my own will but the will of the one who sent me" (5:30). As disciples who believe that Jesus is with us, we can say the same, that we seek the will of the one who sent us.

✠ *What can I learn from this passage?*

The witness to Jesus (5:31–47)

Like Jesus, we have our works to perform. For one brief period in God's creation, we have an opportunity to reflect the light of Christ so that we may be a lamp shedding Christ's light in the world. The message for us is that we, like Jesus, must realize that we are to place our trust in God and not in human praise. We will encounter many people who seem wise in the eyes of the world, but real truth and wisdom reside in God. We shine God's light on creation by performing the works of God.

✠ *What can I learn from this passage?*

Jesus feeds five thousand men (6:1–15)

The feeding of the five thousand in the desert is symbolic of the Eucharist. Jesus sees a large crowd coming toward him, a hungry crowd. In the Eucharist, Jesus daily views millions of people coming to him with a hunger for spiritual nourishment. How can we feed so many in spiritual need with our limited offerings. We cannot, but Jesus gives us the Eucharist and in it, Jesus takes our weak, limited offerings and provides abundance for a hungering world. The word "Eucharist" means "to give thanks." Jesus feeds us with heavenly food, and for this we give thanks for God's nourishment for a spiritually hungry world.

✠ *What can I learn from this passage?*

PART 2: INDIVIDUAL STUDY (JOHN 6:1–71)

Day 1: Jesus Walks on Water (6:16–21)

Mark and Matthew, after presenting the story of the multiplication of the loaves and fish, continue their narrative with Jesus walking on the water. The author of John's Gospel follows this order in his gospel, perhaps to continue to show the link between the New Covenant and the Passover event. After feeding on the lamb, the people of Israel who traveled with Moses crossed the waters of the great sea as they escaped from Egypt. Unlike the people of Moses' day who walked on dry land through the waters, Jesus walks on the water.

The passage begins with the disciples departing for the other side without Jesus. On their journey, they encounter a strong wind and rough seas. When they were three or four miles out on the sea, they see Jesus walking on the water. This story highlights the divinity of Jesus in several ways. Since only God has power over the elements, Jesus' ability to walk on the water shows his divine power. When the disciples become frightened, Jesus says to them, "It is I" (6:20), which stems from the root *I AM*, referencing God's name spoken to Moses from the burning bush. As the disciples are about to take Jesus into the boat, they suddenly arrive ashore at their intended destination. Some see this event as another miracle in the story.

Lectio Divina

Spend 8 to 10 minutes in silent contemplation of the following passage:

In Jesus' day, the Jews believed that demons dwelled in the depths of the sea and that storms occurred when the demons were in turmoil. When the disciples see Jesus walking on the water, they are afraid. Jesus tells them not to fear and uses the divine greeting, "It is I" (6:20). In the midst of the turmoil in our life, we trust God, who is saying to us, "It is I." Do not be afraid. Jesus can overcome the demons in our life. No matter how overwhelming the storms may be, Jesus walks on water and brings us to safety.

✠ *What can I learn from this passage?*

Day 2: Bread of Life Discourse (6:22–40)

In this passage, Jesus delivers a long discourse about being the bread of life. When the crowd realizes that Jesus and his disciples are no longer on their side of the lake, they set out by boat for Capernaum to find him. On the other side of the lake, they locate Jesus and ask when he arrived in the place. Jesus ignores their question and chides them for not understanding the true meaning of his miracle. He tells them they are seeking him not because they believe but because they want him to provide food for them. The miracle was meant to be a sign that Jesus is present in the Eucharist, but the people look for physical nourishment rather than spiritual food. Jesus tells them that the food they seek will perish, and he adds that he offers them food that will satisfy them for eternal life. Jesus calls himself the Son of Man and states that the Father has set his seal upon him; a reference to the descent of the Holy Spirit upon Jesus at his baptism.

The author of the gospel has Jesus answer a second question posed by the crowd. They ask what they can do to perform the works of God. Jesus answers that they must have faith in him, the one sent by God. They ask for a sign in order for them to believe in him, reminding Jesus that Moses gave their ancestors manna in the desert as a sign (Exodus 16:4ff). Jesus responds that it was not Moses who gave them bread from heaven, but it was his Father who gave them manna and who now gives them true bread from heaven, the bread of God that gives life to the world.

As the story continues, we begin to see similarities between this story and that of the woman at the well. Once Jesus mentions the bread of life, the crowd asks for this bread, just as the woman at the well asked for living water when Jesus mentioned it. This leads the discourse away from the taking of the bread to the message about the bread itself. Jesus tells the crowd that he is the bread of life who will fully satisfy the hunger and thirst of those who truly believe in him. Although the people have seen Jesus and his signs, they still do not believe. Jesus will later praise those who believe in him without having to see signs. Jesus comes to fulfill the will of God, and it is God's will that Jesus lose none of those given to him; those called to be his followers who believe in Jesus as the Son of God.

The promise for all disciples is the gift of eternal life and the resurrection on the last day.

Lectio Divina

Spend 8 to 10 minutes in silent contemplation of the following passage:

Just as Jesus comes to do the will of the one who sent him, so we ought to dedicate ourselves to the will of the Father. If we have faith in Jesus, we have the promise of eternal life as long as we follow Jesus' message. This the will of God for us, to perform the works of Christ and to enjoy eternal life with Jesus.

✠ *What can I learn from this passage?*

Day 3: Jesus Offers His Flesh to Eat (6:41–59)

At this point, John changes the group of questioners from the crowd to the Jews, possibly because they challenge Jesus' words more openly as the discourse continues. No one is supposed to know the origins of the Messiah, yet they claim they know Jesus as the son of Joseph and that they know his parents. They question how he can say he came down from heaven. Jesus commands the Jews to stop their complaining, a reference reminiscent of the period in the desert when the Israelites complained against God. Jesus explains that the only ones who can come to attain faith in him are those whom the Father calls to a share in this gift of faith, the one who will raise them up on the last day. He quotes from Isaiah, magnifying that all believers are "taught by the LORD" (Isaiah 54:13). Those who respond to the Father's call will have faith in Jesus. No one but the Son who is from God has seen the Father, but those who believe in the Son will have eternal life.

Jesus declares that he is the bread of life. Unlike the manna in the desert, which did not prevent the death of those who ate it, the living bread that comes from heaven (Jesus) will bring eternal life to those who receive it. The manna is merely physical bread, while the bread of life, which is Jesus himself, is spiritual food and bread for the journey to eternal life. Jesus shocks his audience when he announces that his bread is his flesh for the life of the world.

John writes that the Jews quarreled among themselves, inquiring how Jesus can give his flesh to eat. Jesus tells them that they will have no life in them (meaning spiritual life) if they do not eat his flesh and drink his blood. The author of the gospel writes at a time when the members of the early Church recognized that the bread and wine become the Body and Blood of Jesus during the Eucharistic Liturgy.

Jesus declares that those who eat and drink his Body and Blood will attain eternal life. The Body and Blood of Jesus are real food and drink because they nourish one's eternal life. Just as Jesus draws his life from the Father, so those who eat the body and drink the blood of Jesus will find eternal life from him. This is the true bread that comes down from heaven, as opposed to the bread of Moses that came from the skies. Unlike the ancestors of the Jews who ate the manna and died, those who feed on the bread of life will live forever. John tells us that Jesus spoke these words in a synagogue at Capernaum.

Lectio Divina

Spend 8 to 10 minutes in silent contemplation of the following passage:

We have the privilege of knowing what Jesus meant when he said that he was the bread of life that came down from heaven. People who have faith in Jesus' words know that Christ is fully present in the Eucharist. At the Last Supper, Jesus gave us his Body and Blood in the form of bread and wine to be celebrated in memory of him. Believing in Jesus' power to be present to us in the Eucharist is a vital and powerful mystery of our faith.

✠ *What can I learn from this passage?*

Day 4: Jesus Words of Eternal Life (6:60–71)

Many of Jesus' disciples, who continue to interpret Jesus' words in a physical sense, find the thought of eating his flesh and drinking his blood too difficult to accept. Jesus asks if these thoughts shake their faith. He questions if they would have faith if they saw the Son of Man ascend to the place he held before, namely, his place with the Father. In several lines of this passage, the author points to the death of Jesus on the cross, and he may be speaking of the whole mystery of salvation when he focuses on the ascension. Jesus informs his listeners that he is not speaking of the flesh but of the spirit, for his words are "spirit and life" (6:63). Yet Jesus acknowledges that some refuse to listen to what he is really saying and do not believe. The author tells us that Jesus knew those who would not believe and who would hand him over to death. The gift of faith, he reminds them, comes from the Father.

These words cause a rift between Jesus and some of the disciples, who now leave him. When Jesus asks the Twelve if they also intend to leave him, Peter speaks on their behalf, exclaiming "to whom shall we go? You have the words of eternal life" (6:68), thus illustrating the commitment of the disciples to Jesus. The author uses the term "the Twelve" (6:71) only in this passage and in a later resurrection passage, "when Thomas, one of the Twelve, was not with them when Jesus came" (20:24). Although Jesus himself has chosen the Twelve, he tells them that he is aware that one of them is a devil. John tells us that Jesus is speaking of Judas, the son of Simon Iscariot, the one from among the Twelve who will betray Jesus.

Lectio Divina

Spend 8 to 10 minutes in silent contemplation of the following passage:

Although the words and demands of Jesus may seem as overwhelming as eating flesh or drinking blood, we must say with the Twelve, "Master, to whom shall we go?" (6:68). Once we accept the reality that Jesus is a God who loves us, we are willing to follow, even when we do not yet understand the direction God is inviting us to take. We may have our doubts, our confusion, our questions, but we trust God enough to say, "Lord, to whom shall we go? You have the words of eternal life."

✠ *What can I learn from this passage?*

Review Questions

1. What does Jesus' ability to walk on water signify for the gospel writer?

2. What does Jesus means when he says, "Whoever eats my flesh and drinks my blood remains in me and I in him" (6:56)?

3. Why did some of Jesus' disciples abandon him?

4. What prompted Peter and the Twelve to continue to follow Jesus?

Jesus and the Father Are One

JOHN 7:1—9:41

"Let anyone who thirsts come to me and drink. Whoever believes in me, as scripture says: 'Rivers of living water will flow from within him'" (7:38).

Opening Prayer (SEE PAGE 18)

Context

Part 1: John 7:1—8:11 Jesus goes up to Jerusalem secretly, and when he arrives he astonishes those gathered with his scriptural knowledge, declaring that he has been sent by the Father. Many begin to believe in him as the Messiah because of the signs he performed. In this part, Jesus is threatened by the religious leaders, speaks about living water, and preaches forgiveness to a crowd gathered around a woman caught in the act of adultery.

Part 2: John 8:12—9:41 Jesus calls himself the Light of the World, exhorting that the people will realize it is so when he is lifted up, a reference to the crucifixion. Christ thus declares that he is the way to God. He adds that the true children of Abraham are those who follow his example (Abraham's), and warns the religious leaders to be wary of their sinfulness. A man who was born blind is healed by Jesus in these passages and professes to the religious authorities that it was Christ who healed him of his infirmity.

PART 1: GROUP STUDY (JOHN 7:1—8:11)

Read aloud John 7:1—8:11.

7:1-13 Jesus travels to Jerusalem in secret

Jesus moves throughout Galilee more openly than he can in Jerusalem. When his relatives are going up to Jerusalem for the feast of Booths (feast of Tabernacles), Jesus tells them that he does not intend to travel with them to the celebration. The feast of Booths was a yearly harvest feast that lasted seven days. The people prayed each day for rain for the harvest and lit torches in the women's court of the Temple, illuminating a large portion of Jerusalem at night. The central symbols of the feast were water and light. During this time, the people lived in tents to signify their life during the harvest and to recall that they were a pilgrim people with no eternal home on this earth.

The author of the gospel tells us that Jesus had already decided not to travel throughout the region of Judea because some of the Jews wanted to kill him. Because Jerusalem is the center of Judaism, we can presume that when the author speaks of the Jews in this case, he is speaking of the Jewish religious leaders who reside in Jerusalem. Jesus' relatives ridicule him, mockingly urging him to travel with them to Jerusalem so that his disciples can see his works and have faith in him. This lack of faith on the part of Jesus' relatives is also shown in the Gospel of Mark (Mark 6:4), although the Acts of the Apostles explains that some of Jesus' relatives eventually do come to have faith in him (Acts 1:14).

The world, as depicted in John's Gospel, has no use for the things of heaven. Those who are worldly in their attitudes are loved by the world, while those who live with their attitude directed toward eternal life are hated by the world. Jesus tells his relatives to go to the feast without him, since they belong to the world and are loved by the people of the world. He declares that he, on the other hand, is hated by the world because he belongs to heaven. John the Evangelist tells us that Jesus does not go openly to the feast but instead goes secretly. According to John, Jesus is the center of conversation at the feast. Some think he is a good man, while others think he is evil, leading the people away from the Law of

Moses. Due to the religious leaderships' hatred, no one speaks openly about Jesus.

7:14–36 Jesus dialogues with the Jewish people

Halfway through the feast, Jesus enters the Temple area of Jerusalem and amazes the crowd with his teaching. Just as the people of his own hometown asked where he received such authority and knowledge (Mark 6:1–4), the people in Jerusalem wonder the same. Jesus explains that his teachings are not his own, but that they come from the one who sent him. Those who follow the will of God will recognize that Jesus is teaching the true message, while those who seek their own glory instead of the glory of God will not understand Jesus' message. He accuses the Jews of not following the Law given them by Moses, and he asks why they wish to kill him.

The author uses the literary form of a dialogue to present the message Jesus has to teach. As is common in the Gospel of John, Jesus repeats the same message several times within the dialogue. The people accuse Jesus of being possessed, asking who intends to kill him. He asks the people why they should be surprised that he performed a single good work on the Sabbath. He is referring to the healing of the sick man at the Sheep Pool. He reminds them that Moses gave them circumcision (although it actually came from Abraham and the other patriarchs). The necessity of circumcision in the Law was so great that a child was circumcised on the Sabbath if it was the proper time for this ritual. Jesus questions the logic of their objections. If a male can be circumcised on the Sabbath to avoid transgressing the Law of Moses, then how much more should the healing of a whole person take place on the Sabbath? The people of Jesus' day believed that physical healing was a sign of spiritual healing. Jesus tells them to stop interpreting the Law according to external norms but to judge it honestly.

The dialogue continues. The crowds ask each other whether their leaders are beginning to waver in their opposition to Jesus, since they do nothing about his public appearances. They wonder if the authorities recognize Jesus as the Messiah, but they declare that no one knows the origin of the Messiah, whereas they know Jesus' origins. The confusion continues to arise because of the crowd's inability to separate the spiritual from the material. Some know of Jesus' birthplace, but they do not know that

Jesus' origins are in heaven. Jesus states that he comes, not on his own, but from the one who sent him, the one whom they do not know. Because of Jesus' claim that he knows the one who sent him, the Jewish leaders seek to arrest him, but they cannot, because his hour has not yet come. John the Evangelist continues to show that God has perfect control and that no one can perform any action against Jesus unless God permits it.

The people show signs of believing in Jesus when they question whether the Messiah will perform more signs than Jesus. When the Pharisees hear that the people are beginning to believe in Jesus, they send the Temple guards to arrest him. Not only is the author of John's Gospel speaking of the situation during Jesus' life, but he also explains why the Pharisees turned against Christians in the early Church. Christians believed that Jesus was the Messiah, and they believed the signs he had performed definitely pointed to his special mission.

Jesus continues to speak to the people in a spiritual sense while they continue to interpret his words in a material way. He declares he will go to the one who sent him and that the people will look for him but not find him. The people question where he is going, speculating that he is surely not going to the dispersion to teach among the Greeks. The dispersion referred to the Greek-speaking Jewish communities formed earlier by those who fled Israel to escape the invasions of foreign powers into Palestine.

7:37–52 Rivers of living water

Since the feast of Booths centers on water and light, it is appropriate that Jesus should bring water into his message during the festival. He invites those with a spiritual thirst to come to him. Jesus speaks of himself as a font of living water, and he quotes from the Scriptures stating that rivers of living water shall flow from him, though the Scripture text from the Old Testament is not clear. The author adds two commentaries of his own to Jesus' message. He knows that Jesus is speaking of the sacramental baptism of water and the Spirit, and he looks forward to a later time when Jesus will teach that he must go to the Father in order to send the Spirit to them. For that reason, he can say that as yet there was no Spirit. The author of the gospel links the coming of the Holy Spirit with Jesus' death, resurrection, and ascension. He must go to send the Spirit.

Some in the crowd proclaimed that Jesus was the expected prophet, while others said he was the Messiah. Since many others believed that Jesus came from Galilee, a debate arose based on the expectation that the Messiah would come from the line of David and be born in Bethlehem. Ironically, through their ignorance of Jesus' birthplace and lineage, they were reinforcing his claim to be the Messiah as he actually belonged to the line of David and was born in Bethlehem. Because some in the crowd viewed Jesus as a false Messiah, they wanted to arrest him, but no one dared to lay hands on him.

When the guards return to the Pharisees without Jesus in custody, they inform the Pharisees that never before has anyone spoken like Jesus. The Pharisees mock the guards, questioning whether they have been tricked into believing in Jesus. They sarcastically ask the guards if anyone familiar with a study of the Law of Moses agrees with them. The implied answer is that none of the religious authorities studying Law agreed with the guards. The Pharisees looked with contempt on the common people who were not trained in a study of the Scriptures.

Nicodemus, a member of the Sanhedrin who came to Jesus earlier in the gospel, tries to defend Jesus, claiming that no one is condemned by the Law without first being granted a hearing. In response, the Pharisees question whether he is also a Galilean. Since they believe that Jesus' birthplace is in Galilee and not Jerusalem, they are indirectly accusing Nicodemus of being a follower of Jesus. They urge him to look to the Scripture where he will find no mention of the prophet coming from Galilee. The Pharisees are familiar with the Book of Deuteronomy that records the Lord telling Moses, "I will raise up for them a prophet like you from among their kindred" (Deuteronomy 18:18). The people had no idea that the prophet, whom they expected to be the Messiah, would also be divine.

7:53—8:11 The woman caught in adultery

The story of Jesus and the woman caught in adultery is not found in the older manuscripts of John's Gospel, and some translations omit it entirely or set it off in brackets. Jesus goes to the Temple early in the morning and sits down, a position of authority for a teacher. The crowd does not realize at the time that Jesus is about to teach a lesson of God's love for the sinner.

As Jesus is teaching the crowd, the scribes and Pharisees come to Jesus with a woman caught in the act of adultery and ask him to judge whether the woman should be executed. According to the Law of Moses, a woman caught in adultery was to be stoned to death, but Jesus was preaching a message of mercy and forgiveness. They believe they are about to trap Jesus, since he must either deny the Law of Moses or deny his own teaching. Saying nothing, Jesus begins to write on the ground. He may not have written anything significant but may have chosen the action as a simple diversion, but the author does not tell us what Jesus wrote.

After listening to their persistent questioning, Jesus stands and invites the one without sin to cast a stone at the woman, and, bending down again, continues to write on the ground. This passes the quandary back to them. To cast a stone is to declare oneself sinless and filled with pride. Jesus has those who were judging the woman also judge themselves. One by one, the scribes and the Pharisees move away, leaving Jesus alone with the woman. Jesus dialogues with the woman by posing a question to her: "Has no one condemned you?" (8:10). Jesus does not condone her adultery, but he shows his mercy and forgiveness when he tells her to go and to avoid this sin in the future. The story reads as if it could have come from the Gospel of Luke rather than from John's Gospel; and some ancient manuscripts have added this story to Luke's Gospel.

Review Questions

1. Why was Jesus hesitant to go to Jerusalem? According to Jesus, why should good acts be allowed on the Sabbath? Explain.
2. What prompts the crowd to begin to believe in Jesus?
3. What did Jesus mean when he said that living waters would flow from within him? Discuss.
4. Why is Jesus' origin so important to the Jewish leaders?
5. What lessons can we learn from Jesus' forgiveness of the woman taken in adultery?

Closing Prayer (SEE PAGE 18)

Pray the closing prayer now or after *lectio divina*.

Lectio Divina (SEE PAGE 11)

Relax your body and maintain a posture of prayer (back straight, eyes shut, feet flat on the floor). This exercise can take as long as you want, but in the context of this Bible study, 10 to 20 minutes should be sufficient.

The meditations that follow are provided only to help group participants use this prayer form, but note that *lectio* is intended to bring one to a place of prayerful contemplation where the Word of God speaks to the hearer from his or her heart. See page 11 for further instruction.

Jesus travels to Jerusalem in secret (7:1–13)

In Matthew, Jesus tells his disciples when he sends them on a mission to be "shrewd as serpents and simple as doves" (Matthew 10:16). Jesus goes to Jerusalem secretly because he knows that the religious leaders wish to arrest him. Although he remains as simple as a dove, he is as cunning as a serpent. This example of Jesus is to help Christians profess faith in Christ and be as wise as serpents in order to prevent some greater evil. Being a follower of Jesus calls us to share Christ's message by following his example of simplicity and wisdom.

✠ *What can I learn from this passage?*

Jesus dialogues with the Jewish people (7:14–36)

Jesus declares he is following the law of God by healing on the Sabbath, and he teaches that it is in conformity with God's law to perform good deeds at all times. Jesus teaches that we are called to perform good acts every day of our life without exception. This message and these deeds come from Jesus, who is God.

✠ *What can I learn from this passage?*

Rivers of living water (7:37–52)

Many in the world thirst for an answer to the anxieties and fears they face in life without realizing that they really thirst for faith. Jesus calls all people who thirst to come to him as the river of living water. Baptism bestows the Holy Spirit on those celebrating the sacrament, a gift from God. Because we know that Jesus is the Messiah, we trust his words and accept in faith that the gift of the Spirit comes to us through baptism. Just as the Spirit guided Jesus through his life, so the Spirit will guide us through ours.

✠ *What can I learn from this passage?*

The woman caught in adultery (7:53—8:11)

Jesus continues to correct an understanding of the Law of Moses by showing us that God is a loving, compassionate, and forgiving God. Jesus is more concerned with the future than with the past. The woman taken in adultery is to go and sin no more. The purpose of forgiveness is not to punish a person but to invite the person to live a life free from sin. Jesus says to all people who seek forgiveness of sins, no matter how great they may be, "Go, and from now on do not sin any more" (8:11).

✠ *What can I learn from this passage?*

PART 2: INDIVIDUAL STUDY (JOHN 8:12—9:41)

Day 1: Jesus, the Light of the World (8:12–20)

As mentioned earlier in this commentary, the central themes of the feast of Booths (Tabernacles) are water and light. Jesus has already given a discourse concerning the living water. He now speaks of himself as the Light of the World, claiming that his followers will escape the darkness of a sinful world and will walk in the light of life. The Pharisees confront Jesus, claiming that he cannot be preaching the truth since he has no witnesses to support him. According to Jewish law, a person must have at least two witnesses to vouch for any message being taught. Jesus answers that because he has come from the Father and will go to the Father, no human being can be a witness to the message he preaches. Only the one sent and the one sending can be a witness to the words of Jesus. Jesus asserts that he and the Father suffice as witnesses to judge what he is saying, accusing the Pharisees of judging by human standards. Since their law demands two witnesses to the truth, Jesus is saying that he has two witnesses, namely himself and the Father.

The Pharisees ask where Jesus' Father is. Jesus tells them that if they knew who he was, they would also know the Father. Because Jesus challenges those who are supposed to interpret the law, he could expect the insulted Pharisees to arrest him, but they are not able to take him, since his hour had not yet come.

Lectio Divina

Spend 8 to 10 minutes in silent contemplation of the following passage:

When we understand that Jesus and the Father are one, we recognize that Jesus is indeed the Light of the World who speaks with the authority of God. As Christians, we not only view the world in a material sense, but we look beyond the world through the light of faith, enabling us to see Jesus as a guiding light. If we accept Jesus' testimony, we live by faith with the belief that his message is the message of God for all people.

✠ *What can I learn from this passage?*

Day 2: Jesus Foretells His Death (8:21–30)

Jesus informs his listeners that he will go away where they cannot come because of their sinfulness. They continue to interpret Jesus' words in a human sense, thinking that perhaps he intends to commit suicide. Ironically, although he does not intend to commit suicide, he does intend, by his own free will, to offer himself in sacrifice for the sins of the world. Jesus tells his audience that they belong to the world, while he belongs to the things that are above. The world in which the Pharisees live cannot have power over Jesus. He warns his listeners that they will die in their sins unless they come to believe him when he proclaims, "I AM" (8:24). This is a clear reference to Jesus' claim to oneness in God and is reminiscent of the term God used when speaking to Moses from the burning bush (Exodus 3:14).

Jesus claims that since the beginning he has been telling them about himself, but they refuse to hear his words. He could say much in judgment of them, but he states only those things he hears from God. Jesus speaks of his unity as well as his dependence on the Father's will. When Jesus recognizes their lack of understanding, he tells them that they will recognize him as I AM when he is lifted up. This is a reference again to the total mystery of Christ's death, resurrection, and ascension. When these things occur, they will recognize that Christ is indeed one with the Father who sent him and with the one whose voice he hears. Because of his faithfulness to the Father, he knows the Father will never abandon him. Many people believe in Jesus because of his words, but their faith is shallow, as will become evident.

Lectio Divina

Spend 8 to 10 minutes in silent contemplation of the following passage:

Jesus' longing is always to be with his Father, but he has come to fulfill the will of the Father. The realization that the Son of God took flesh and dwelt among us is far beyond the understanding of those who are concerned only with things of earth. In light of Jesus' message about his unity with the Father, people of faith live on earth believing that there is more to life than is seen by the eye.

✠ *What can I learn from this passage?*

Day 3: True Children of Abraham (8:31–47)

Jesus informs the Jewish leaders that they would be his disciples if they lived according to his message and that they would then know the truth that will set them free, no longer subject to the powers of this world. The word "free" leads the Pharisees to protest that they are true children of Abraham and have never been slaves to anyone. They ask Jesus how he can say that they will become free when they are already free. Jesus responds that those who live in sin are slaves of sin and their sinfulness severs them from the household. Slaves do not have the right to live permanently with the family, but the son does. If the son frees them from slavery, then they are free. Jesus is telling them that sinners who live in the family of Abraham are no better than slaves. Although they belong to the family of Abraham, the words of Jesus are rejected by the Jews who want to kill him. Jesus warns them that his message comes from his Father in heaven, and he accuses the Jewish leaders of acting according to the guidance of their own father, the devil.

When the Pharisees retort that Abraham is their father, Jesus rejects their response, stating that if they were Abraham's children, they would be doing the work of Abraham, but they are attempting to kill him for telling the truth that comes from God. Jesus' condemnation angers the Pharisees, and they claim that they are not illegitimate but true children of the one God who is their Father. The Jews considered those who followed false gods or more than one god as illegitimate children. Jesus does not accept their objection, stating that they would love him, the true Son, if they knew the true God and Father. Because they have chosen to close their ears to the words of Jesus, they have chosen the devil, the father of death and deceitfulness and one who does not speak the truth. Jesus informs them that because he speaks the truth, they refuse to believe him. He challenges them to tell him how he has sinned and asks them why they do not listen to him when he speaks the truth. Those who belong to God hear the words of God, but since they do not belong to God, they do not listen. Jesus continues to speak on the spiritual level, while the religious leaders listen on the worldly level.

Lectio Divina

Spend 8 to 10 minutes in silent contemplation of the following passage:

> Those who accept the truth find freedom in their faith in Jesus. It is not a worldly freedom but a spiritual freedom that enables them to recognize that God is with them. Those who follow Jesus and his law of love are free and more capable of understanding his message, whereas those who sin become so possessed by sin that they cannot understand the ways of God.

✠ *What can I learn from this passage?*

Day 4: Jesus Does Not Seek His Own Glory (8:48–59)

The Jews try to insult Jesus by stating that he is possessed and that he thinks the way the hated Samaritans do. Although the author of the Gospel of John realizes at the time of the writing that many of the Samaritans have converted to Christ, he presents his message from the viewpoint of the Judeans of Jesus' day. At the time of writing this gospel, there were still some people of Judea who hated the Samaritans. Jesus' accusers link being a Samaritan with possession.

Jesus denies being possessed and tells them that he respects his Father, but they refuse to respect him (Jesus). What they judge to be possession is Jesus' faithfulness to the will of God, which they do not understand. As John has already told us, they see only appearances. Because Jesus has no apparent regard for the Sabbath, they believe he is possessed. Jesus does not seek his own glory, but his Father seeks to glorify the Son. Those faithful to the teachings of Jesus will inherit eternal life and will never see death. Jesus emphasizes this statement by adding the words, "Amen, amen, I say to you" (8:51).

The conflict of views continues as the Jews again interpret Jesus' words in a worldly sense, rather than seeing them as Jesus intended. They interpret death as physical and claim that Jesus must be possessed to state that a person would never die. Even their great ancestor Abraham died, as did the prophets. They ask Jesus if he is greater than these. The reader of the Gospel of John knows that the answer to this question is "Yes."

Jesus declares that he does not seek his own glory, since it would come to nothing, but his Father seeks to glorify him. They do not know God, although they claim they do know God. Jesus must profess that he knows God; otherwise he would be a liar like his adversaries. He tells them that Abraham longed to see the day of his coming, and he rejoiced when he saw it. This does not mean that Abraham saw the coming of Christ directly, but that he realized that God's covenant would be fulfilled at the moment his wife gave birth to his son Isaac (Genesis 17:17). Abraham knew that his line would continue as God had promised.

In Jesus' time, a fifty-year-old person was considered to be enjoying old age. The Jews question how Jesus, who is not yet fifty, can claim to have seen Abraham. Jesus answers with a direct claim of divinity, telling them that before Abraham existed, "I Am" (8:58). Because he uses the same expression for himself as God used with Moses when he appeared to him in a burning bush (Exodus 3:14), the Jews pick up stones to hurl at Jesus. Stoning was the penalty for blasphemy, and they sought to kill Jesus because he claimed equality with God. Because the hour had not yet come for Jesus to be killed, he again is able to slip away and leave the Temple.

Lectio Divina

Spend 8 to 10 minutes in silent contemplation of the following passage:

> The religious leaders refused to hear Jesus' words. He was speaking the truth, but they could not accept the truth because they could not accept Jesus. Jesus is the visible image of the invisible God who does not seek his own glory, but the glory of the one who sent him. In our liturgy, we pray in the name of Jesus, the Son of God, and our prayer is directed to God the Father. All our prayers end as we pray through Christ, our Lord. Jesus came to bring glory to the Father, and this he does through the prayers of the liturgy.

✠ *What can I learn from this passage?*

Day 5: The Man Born Blind (9:1–59)

In the Book of Exodus, God warns the people that he is a jealous God and that children to the third and fourth generation will be punished for the wickedness of their fathers (Exodus 20:5). The Jews interpreted the text to mean that physical illness of any type was a sign of God's punishment not only on those who sin but also on their offspring. When Jesus and his disciples encounter a blind man, the disciples ask Jesus whether this man is suffering for his own sins or for the sins of his father. They significantly call Jesus "Rabbi" in this exchange, a term used for one who is a teacher. Jesus responds that neither this man nor his father has sinned, thus implying that physical illness is not a sign of God's displeasure. He declares that the blindness of this particular man has a purpose. His cure is a sign that the light of the world is present in Jesus as he gives physical and spiritual sight to the man born blind. The power of darkness does not yet have its hold over the fate of Jesus, who must let his light shine forth in the world while there is still time.

The cure of the blind man recalls images used during the sacrament of baptism in the early Church. Anointing with oil takes place in the celebration of baptism. Jesus anoints the eyes of the blind man with mud. The practice of smearing mud on a person during a healing was a common practice in Jesus' day. The anointing with mud has a deeper significance for those who recognize it as the baptismal anointing. Jesus tells the man to go to the Pool of Siloam to wash, another reference to baptism. The name Siloam means "sent," a term John the Evangelist often uses in referring to Jesus in this Gospel. Jesus is sent by the Father. When the man washes in the waters, he regains his sight and begins a journey toward spiritual light.

When his neighbors and others who knew the healed man as the blind beggar see him, they argue among themselves, some saying he is the man born blind, while others believe he is someone else. The man becomes a witness for Jesus, stating that he has indeed received his sight from the one they call Jesus. When the people bring the blind man to the Pharisees, the religious leaders begin to argue among themselves. Some contend that because Jesus cured the blind man on the Sabbath, he could not be from God. Others object, saying that God would not allow a sinner to perform such signs. When they ask the blind man his opinion of Jesus, the man professes faith in Christ, declaring, "He is a prophet!"

The Pharisees, who refuse to believe that this man had truly been born blind, summon the man's parents, who acknowledge that the man is their son and that he was born blind, but they are afraid to answer any further questions. They tell the Pharisees to ask their son how he received his sight. John tells us that the leaders of the Jews had already decided that anyone who professed faith in Christ would be expelled from the synagogue. This reference to expulsion from the synagogue did not exist in Jesus' time, but it did become a law toward the end of the first century. During the time when the author was writing this gospel, those who professed faith in Christ were expelled from the synagogues.

The Pharisees call the man before them again and tell him to glorify God rather than Jesus. They spoke as the official authority of Judaism when they declared that Jesus, in their view, was a sinner. The blind man stands firm, stating that he does not know whether Jesus is a sinner; all he knows is that he was once blind, and Jesus gave him sight. When they ask the blind man to tell them again what had happened, the blind man chides them, asking if they want to become disciples of Jesus. It is obvious from this passage that the blind man has become a follower of Jesus. The Pharisees claim to follow Moses, but they declare that they have no idea about Jesus' origins. This recalls an earlier debate between Jesus and those Jews who stated that no one would know the origins of the Messiah. The healed man expresses surprise that the Pharisees do not know where Jesus comes from, yet Jesus gave him sight. As leaders of the people, they are expected to know everything. The man states that Jesus must be from God, since they all know that God would not allow a sinner to perform such deeds. The man's words insult the leaders, and they reprimand him, reminding him that his blindness was proof that he was born in sin, yet here he is trying to teach them; then they throw the man out of the Temple.

Jesus finds the blind man and asks if he believes in the Son of Man. When the man asks who he is, Jesus tells him, "The one speaking to you is he." The man declares that he does believe, a response that is not found in the oldest manuscripts. Jesus proclaims that he has come so that those without sight may see, that is, to give faith to those who are spiritually blind. He adds that he will make blind those who think they have sight; he will not be able to reach them because they arrogantly reject Jesus' words. When the Pharisees ask Jesus if he is including them among the blind, Jesus tells them that those who are blind and do not know God are not as sinful as those who claim to have faith yet remain in sin. The reference is to the Pharisees who believe they have faith in God, but since they are self righteous, they are blind.

The story of the healing of the man who was blind from birth is an excellent story of progressive faith. The man first acknowledges Jesus as a prophet, then as the one sent by God, and finally as the Son of Man. From beginning to end, he struggles to understand who Jesus is, and his faith progressively grows. Each new encounter shows that he is gaining a greater insight into Jesus, the Light of the World.

Lectio Divina

Spend 8 to 10 minutes in silent contemplation of the following passage:

At the beginning of one's faith journey, some are distressed by those who challenge their faith. In this story about the blind man, he becomes more firm in his faith in Jesus, just as a new believer may do. Finally, he receives instruction and encouragement from Jesus. Instruction and encouragement are important elements for those seeking to establish a firm foundation in the faith. As our faith grows, it follows a gradual process that will reach fulfillment when we share in the resurrection.

✠ *What can I learn from this passage?*

Review Questions

1. What did Jesus mean when he said, "Where I am going, you cannot come?"
2. How will the people recognize Jesus as "I AM" when he is lifted up?
3. What does Jesus mean when he says that Abraham rejoiced to see Jesus' day?
4. Explain the significance of Jesus' healing of the man born blind?

The Approach of Jesus' Hour

JOHN 10:1—12:50

Jesus said to her, "(Martha), I am the resurrection and the life; whoever believes in me, even if he dies, will live, and everyone who lives and believes in me will never die. Do you believe this?" She said to him, "Yes, Lord, I have come to believe that you are the Messiah, the Son of God, the one who is coming into the world" (11:25–27).

Opening Prayer (SEE PAGE 18)

Context

Part 1: John 10:1—11:44 In these passages, Jesus identifies himself as a sheep gate (the way to God), and makes known that he is the good shepherd who calls his followers (sheep) to recognize his voice (message). The Jewish leaders are hostile toward Jesus, who claims that he does the will of the Father. Also, Jesus learns that Lazarus has died and goes to the home of Martha and Mary. After Martha professes that Jesus is the Messiah, the Son of God, he raises Lazarus from the dead.

Part 2: John 11:45—12:50 The Sanhedrin seek to kill Jesus after learning that he raised Lazarus from the dead. Caiaphas, the high priest, unwittingly makes a prophetic statement about Jesus by declaring that one man should die instead of the people. Now that the religious leaders planned to kill Jesus, he must travel in secret. He goes up to Bethany six days before Passover, and Mary, the sister of Lazarus, anoints his feet with costly perfume. When others become upset with this act, Jesus responds that she is anointing him for his burial. Jesus enters Jerusalem amid a glorious welcome and declares that the hour is coming when he will be lifted up.

PART 1: GROUP STUDY (JOHN 10:1—11:44)

Read aloud John 10:1—11:44.

10:1–21 The Good Shepherd

Although John's Gospel, unlike the synoptic Gospels, does not make use of parables, the opening lines of this chapter are considered by many as a type of parable. Besides writing about the situation surrounding Jesus at this time, the author also plants many subtle messages in the story that could apply to conditions in the Church during the era in which he was writing. The background for the message about the Good Shepherd comes from the Old Testament prophet Ezekiel (Ezekiel 34:1–31). Ezekiel tells of the leaders of the people of his own day taking advantage of their position and caring for their own desires at the expense of the people. God will deprive them of their authority and will become the shepherd of the people. He will send another shepherd who will be like David. In the Gospel of John, this new shepherd is Jesus Christ.

Jesus first speaks about entering the sheepfold through the gate. Only those who wish to steal the sheep would have to enter another way to bypass the one who tends the gate. The one who tends the gate knows the true shepherd and allows him to enter. As shepherds traveled throughout different territories during Jesus' day, they would leave their sheep in a pen with other sheep. In the morning, the shepherd would call the sheep, who would recognize his voice and follow him. The other sheep would remain in the pen, awaiting the familiar voice of their own shepherd.

When Jesus realizes that the people do not understand his message, he continues his discourse. He says, "I am the gate for the sheep." The way to safely enter the sheepfold is through Jesus Christ. The religious leaders who fatten themselves by taking advantage of the people are thieves and robbers. Jesus is speaking to the people of his own day, while John the Evangelist may be conveying a message directed at the leaders of the early Church who misuse their authority.

Jesus calls himself the Good Shepherd. This recalls Psalm 23, which speaks of the Lord as a shepherd. Unlike the one who is hired, the good shepherd protects the sheep and even goes so far as to lay down his life for them. Jesus is alluding to his own death on behalf of his sheep. Those who are faithful to God will recognize the voice of Christ as their true shepherd, and they will follow Christ. Others who do not belong to the original fold will also follow Christ. This may be a reference to the gentiles who accept Jesus much more readily than the Jewish people. All distinctions will disappear for those who follow Jesus. There will be one fold that follows the one shepherd, Jesus Christ. The Father loves the Son who lays down his life freely and made the choice to offer himself for the sheep. The Father has given the Son the power to lay down his life and to take it up again (resurrection and ascension). In doing so, Jesus is faithful to the Father's will.

When Jesus finishes his discourse, the people begin to argue among themselves, some claiming that Jesus is possessed and unworthy of any attention, while others claim that his words and actions cannot be those of a possessed man.

10:22–42 Feast of Dedication

In the First Book of Maccabees, we read of the struggle of the Jewish people under the leadership of Judas Maccabeus against a foreign ruler named Antiochus Epiphanes, who placed a statue of Zeus in the Jewish Temple. Judas Maccabeus led a revolt against the foreign ruler and cleansed the Temple of its foreign gods, rededicating it to the Lord (1 Maccabees 4:36ff). Each year the Jews celebrate the feast of this event in mid-December at the feast of Hanukkah. Like the feast of Tabernacles, it lasts several days and is centered on the lights that lit up Jerusalem during the rededication of the Temple.

During the celebration of the feast of Dedication, Jesus was walking in an area of the Temple called Solomon's Portico which was on the east side and which provided protection against the cold winds of the desert. The Acts of the Apostles tells us that it was a popular meeting place for the members of the early Church community (see Acts 5:12). In the first chapter of the Gospel of John, emissaries from the priests and Levites ask the Baptist who he is, and John replies that he is not the Messiah (1:20). The Jews now beg Jesus not to keep them in suspense but to tell them openly whether or not he is the Messiah.

Jesus declares that he has already answered their question, but they refused to accept what he was telling them. Although Jesus has declared his unity with the Father, the religious leaders are not able to understand the symbolism involved in his message. They are looking for visible signs and a clear message that he is the Messiah. The belief in Jesus' day was that the Messiah would come and restore the Temple. Since the feast of Dedication is the feast of the restoration of the Temple, it was a fitting question to ask on such an occasion.

John links this episode of the feast of Dedication with Jesus' previous discourse about the Good Shepherd. Jesus tells his audience that his works, done in God's name, witness to his mission, but those who are not his sheep reject them. He already told them that he was "I AM" and the Messiah. His sheep, however, have listened, and they are sharing in eternal life because they have chosen to hear his message and follow him. They do not have to ask him to speak plainly, because they believe, and for them, he has spoken plainly. The sheep hear the voice of the Good Shepherd. Because his sheep also belong to the Father, they will never be destroyed or snatched away from the Son. Jesus again expresses his unity with the Father by stating that he and the Father are one.

The Jews, understanding the words of Jesus as a claim to divinity, pick up stones to hurl at him. Jesus demands to know what good deeds have provoked them to stone him. When they inform him that they want to stone him because he is making himself equal to God, Jesus challenges their interpretation of his words. He alludes to Psalm 82:6, where God calls the Judges "gods," sons of the Most High. Jesus refers to this psalm as their Law. For most Jews, every part of the Scriptures is the Law, not simply the Book of the Law, the first five books of the Bible. If they can accept the judges as gods, then how can they turn on the true Son whom

God has sent into the world? Jesus invites them to judge his works. If they are not the Father's works, then they should refuse to believe in him, but if they are the Father's works, then they should recognize that he is in the Father and the Father is in him. They again try to arrest Jesus but are unable to do so. Implied in their inability to arrest him is the fact that Jesus' hour has not yet come.

In contrast to Jesus' poor reception in Jerusalem, John tells us that the people across the Jordan flock to Jesus when he returns there. This was the place that John the Baptist used to baptize. The followers of the Baptist profess faith in Jesus, noting that the Baptist never performed any miracles, but that everything he said about Jesus was true.

11:1–44 The death of Lazarus

The story of raising Lazarus from the dead becomes part of a transitional narrative that leads from Jesus' public ministry to his death and resurrection. The author tells us that Jesus receives word that Lazarus, whom he loves, is sick and near death. Lazarus is the brother of Martha and Mary, both of whom also appear in the Gospel of Luke, but Luke makes no reference to a brother of Martha and Mary (Luke 10:38–42). Upon receiving the news of Lazarus' sickness, Jesus foretells that the sickness will not end in death but instead will lead to the glorification of the Son. This may be a reference to the glory given Jesus as he raises Lazarus from the dead, but likely also points beyond the death and rising of Lazarus to Jesus' glorification in his own resurrection.

Jesus waits two days before returning to Judea. His disciples, remembering that Jesus had recently escaped from Judea to avoid the people of the area who wanted to stone him, protest that Jesus will place himself in danger if he returns to Judea. In answer to his disciples, Jesus makes a veiled reference to his hour of glorification. Because the hour has not yet begun, Jesus is free to walk in the midst of the people. Jesus reminds his listeners that there are twelve hours of light in a day (the number of hours that the Jewish people considered to be daylight). So, Jesus draws a spiritual message from this image of light. As long as Jesus walks in the light of God's protection, no one can touch him, but he knows that the hour of darkness and the cross will eventually arrive.

Jesus tells his disciples that Lazarus has fallen asleep, meaning that he has died. The disciples misunderstand Jesus and see sleep as a sign that Lazarus is regaining his health. When Jesus states bluntly that Lazarus has died, he adds that he is about to perform a sign that will lead the disciples to a deeper faith. Thomas calls on his fellow disciples to join him in going to die with Jesus, a statement that forms a foundation for true discipleship. In the early Church, many of those who professed faith in Jesus were put to death for preaching Jesus' message. Thomas himself did not realize the total truth of his statement, namely that many would die for Jesus down through the ages.

When Jesus arrives with his disciples at Bethany, a village about two miles from Jerusalem, Martha runs out to meet him. She expresses her faith in the healing power of Jesus, stating that Lazarus would not have died if Jesus had been there. Her faith is expansive. She knows Jesus can heal the sick, and she hints to Jesus that he can still do something about the death of Lazarus. When Jesus tells Martha that Lazarus will rise again, Martha expresses her belief in the resurrection of the dead on the last day. Jesus responds by calling himself "the resurrection and the life," that is, he is the living resurrection and life for those who believe in him. Those who remain faithful will share in Christ's resurrection as long as they continue to have faith in him. In his debate with Martha, Jesus is not speaking about physical death but about spiritual death. In response, Martha, in John's Gospel, has the privilege of expressing a profession of faith found on the lips of Peter in the synoptic Gospels: "I believe that you are the Messiah, the Son of God, the one coming into the world."

After speaking with Jesus, Martha secretly tells Mary that Jesus has arrived, and Mary runs out to meet him. She too states that Lazarus would not have died if Jesus had been present. Jesus, responding with emotion, asks where they have laid the body, and he goes to the tomb. The people are amazed at Jesus' weeping, and they wonder why he did not heal Lazarus as he had healed the blind man. This episode shows that Jesus is already well-known among the people as a miracle worker. When Jesus orders the stone covering the tomb to be taken away, Martha protests that Lazarus has been dead four days and the smell of decay will already be present. In

Jewish thought, a person was considered truly dead after three days. Since Lazarus has been dead four days, no one could doubt his death.

Jesus praises the Father for hearing him and for using this occasion to witness that he is truly sent by God. He himself has no doubt that God hears his prayers, but Jesus knows that the people lack faith in him. Jesus calls Lazarus from the tomb, and Lazarus comes forth, bound in a burial cloth. The miracle is a sign given for the sake of the people. It points beyond the raising of Lazarus from the dead to Jesus' mission and his own death and resurrection. At Jesus' orders, the people free Lazarus from his bindings. The message speaks to the bonds of spiritual death, namely sin, and it reminds us that Jesus comes to free all sinners from these bonds. The story ends abruptly, but the author continues with the resulting effects of the miracle on the leaders of the Jewish people.

Some commentators believe that Lazarus was the one identified as the "beloved disciple," since the passage begins with the author of the gospel stating that "Jesus loved Martha and her sister and Lazarus." The beloved disciple is not really identified as the Apostle John, nor one of the Twelve.

Review Questions

1. How do you understand the two messages found in the story of the Good Shepherd?
2. How does Jesus respond to the religious leaders concerning his identity as the Messiah?
3. Explain Martha's role in the raising of Lazarus from the dead. Why is it important?
4. Why is Jesus troubled at the death of Lazarus?
5. What is significant about Jesus raising Lazarus from the dead?

Closing Prayer (SEE PAGE 18)

Pray the closing prayer now or after *lectio divina*.

Lectio Divina (SEE PAGE 11)

Relax your body and maintain a posture of prayer (back straight, eyes shut, feet flat on the floor). This exercise can take as long as you want, but in the context of this Bible study, 10 to 20 minutes should be sufficient.

The meditations that follow are provided only to help group participants use this prayer form, but note that *lectio* is intended to bring one to a place of prayerful contemplation where the Word of God speaks to the hearer from his or her heart. See page 11 for further instruction.

The Good Shepherd (10:1–21)

Some who claim to believe in Jesus but do not put his message into action are like the hired hands who flee when any opposition to their faith in Christ arises. Jesus is the gate, the way to eternal life; the Good Shepherd who passes his ministry on to us. As baptized Christians, we are no longer the hired hands but a people who share in the life of the Good Shepherd and act on his behalf. Our words and our deeds are the gates through which people meet Christ.

✠ *What can I learn from this passage?*

Feast of Dedication (10:22–42)

Jesus tells us that the works he performs, he performs in his Father's name and that he and the Father are one. As members of Jesus' sheepfold who follow him, we are able to hear and understand his message as a message from God, while those who do not belong to the sheepfold of Christ can hear his message and lack the faith necessary to understand it. Once we belong to the sheepfold and trust Christ, he promises to protect us. Living with this belief, we produce good fruit as Jesus did.

✠ *What can I learn from this passage?*

The Death of Lazarus (11:1–44)

When Lazarus comes out of the tomb, Jesus commands the people to untie him and let him go, just as Jesus commands unclean spirits to lose their control over those who were spiritually dead. The story reflects God's love in freeing people from their demons and illustrates the power of prayer.

✠ *What can I learn from this passage?*

PART 2: INDIVIDUAL STUDY (JOHN 11:45—12:50)

Day 1: The Plot to Kill Jesus (11:45–57)

The crowd reacts to the incident of Jesus' raising Lazarus from the dead in different ways. Some believe in Jesus, while others go to the Pharisees and report what Jesus has done. Jewish leaders meet in the Sanhedrin and express their fears that the signs Jesus is performing will soon lead the whole world to become his followers. They realize the Romans will not tolerate a religious leader who is a threat to their rule, and the religious leaders fear that Roman soldiers will overrun Jerusalem and the Temple. The readers of the Gospel of John know that Jerusalem and the Temple had already been destroyed long before this gospel was written. Since Caiaphas was high priest that year, the author of the gospel states that Caiaphas actually prophesied that Jesus was about to die for the nation, but not in the sense intended by Caiaphas. Jesus would die, not only for the nation, but for the unity of all the dispersed children of God.

Because the leaders now seek an occasion to kill Jesus, he leaves for Ephraim, a desert area ten to fifteen miles northeast of Jerusalem. With Passover only a few days away, a large number of pilgrims swarm into Jerusalem for the feast, wondering whether Jesus will show himself. The chief priests and the Pharisees now show open hostility toward Jesus, and they order the people to report to them if they see Jesus so that they can arrest him.

Lectio Divina

Spend 8 to 10 minutes in silent contemplation of the following passage:

As Christians, we know that Jesus died for all people, not just to save the people of Israel. Ironically, Caiaphus unintentionally prophesies concerning Jesus. The death of Jesus brings salvation to the whole world, and Caiaphus prophesied that Christ would die for the nation. However, his meaning was other than what he intended. As sad as the death of Jesus was, Jesus accepted the Father's will that it was better for him to die for the salvation of the world than to let all people suffer spiritual death. This was acceptable to God's great love for all people.

✠ *What can I learn from this passage?*

Day 2: Mary Anoints Jesus (12:1–11)

As John began his gospel by describing the first week of Jesus' ministry, he now draws it to a close by describing the last week of Jesus' ministry. Six days before Passover, Jesus arrives in Bethany, the village where Lazarus was raised from the dead. Martha is serving while Mary comes to Jesus with expensive perfumed oil, anoints his feet with it, and dries them with her hair. Washing and anointing the feet of a guest was usually the duty of a slave. The expensive ointment points to the sacred position of Jesus in the mind of Mary.

In the synoptic Gospels, we read about similar anointings that likely had their source in the same literary traditions (Mark 14:1–11; Matthew 26:6–13; Luke 7:36–50). In Luke's Gospel, we learn that the woman who anointed Jesus' feet was a known sinner, and this has led some commentators to identify Mary as that sinful woman, although John does not make this connection. Likewise, this mistaken connection led some to identify Mary in this story with Mary Magdalene. There is, however, no real evidence linking the two.

Judas appears in this episode as an open opponent of the anointing, claiming that the ointment could have been sold and the money given to the poor. The author tells us that the real intent of Judas was to keep the money for himself. Linking the anointing with a prophecy of his burial, Jesus orders his disciples to allow Mary to continue. The ointment she uses is apparently the same oil used for burials. In answer to Judas' protest, Jesus teaches that the poor will always be present. He is not making a statement for or against our need to alleviate poverty; he is stating that all human needs must be served in correct fashion. Some in Jesus' era believed that the appropriate burial of the dead was a fundamental condition for resurrection and was a greater act of mercy over almsgiving.

Crowds of people come to see Jesus and Lazarus, whom he had raised from the dead. Because the Pharisees notice that many of the people were leaving Judaism to follow Jesus because of Lazarus whom he had raised from the dead, the Pharisees wanted to kill Lazarus along with Jesus. For the readers of John's Gospel, the intent of the Pharisees to kill Lazarus, a follower of Jesus, would also apply to the early Church period when Jesus' followers were enduring persecution.

Lectio Divina

Spend 8 to 10 minutes in silent contemplation of the following passage:

As Jesus' death draws near, he knows he will be buried in haste. He praises Mary for anointing him and applies her action to his burial, while Judas shows the power earthly wealth has over him illustrated in his reaction to Mary's actions. The story challenges us to identify where we are in our relationship to Jesus. Mary took the position of humility, serving Jesus by anointing his feet as though she were a slave. Jesus challenges us to determine whether service or a desire to live a life of luxury at all costs determines how we live. The true follower of Christ chooses to accept the role of serving others, as Mary did.

✠ *What can I learn from this passage?*

Day 3: Triumphal Entry Into Jerusalem (12:12–19)

The next day, five days before Passover, the crowds gather palm branches and go out to meet Jesus for his triumphal entry into Jerusalem. The synoptic Gospels tell of Jesus' triumphant entry into Jerusalem (Mark 11:1–10; Matthew 21:1–11; Luke 19:29–40), but only in John's Gospel do we read that the enthusiasm of the crowd is due to the miracle of raising Lazarus from the dead. In the synoptic Gospels, the people pick up branches to greet Jesus, but John tells us that they used palm branches.

The people cry out their "Hosanna!" to Jesus, using Psalm 118:25–26 as their prayer of triumph for him. The author quotes from the prophet Zechariah (Zechariah 9:9) in proclaiming that the king shall come in humility and service, riding upon a donkey. Only after the resurrection of Jesus did his disciples realize that Jesus was fulfilling this prophecy. The proclamation of Jesus as king is a central issue in the coming passion. The

Pharisees, who feel helpless against Jesus, are disturbed that the whole world is turning toward him. At the time John the Evangelist wrote this gospel, Jesus' message was spreading rapidly throughout the known world, far beyond the borders of Israel.

Lectio Divina

Spend 8 to 10 minutes in silent contemplation of the following passage:

In spiritual growth, people sometimes experience a short period of consolation as praying becomes easy and God seems so close; a Palm Sunday of the spiritual life. On the spiritual journey, God may seem to disappear, even to the point of leading some to have grave doubts about the reality of God. Prayer becomes difficult and filled with distractions. This spiritual struggle could become the Good Friday of one's spiritual journey. The spiritual life is filled with Palm Sundays and Good Fridays until the day when God finally calls us to our eternal Easter Sunday.

✠ *What can I learn from this passage?*

Day 4: The Grain of Wheat Must Die (12:20–26)

Some Greeks approach Philip, asking to speak to Jesus. Philip goes to Andrew, and together they approach the Lord. As the narrative continues, Greeks and Jews come to Jesus through his disciples rather than directly. At the time of the writing of this gospel, the message of Jesus is spreading throughout the Greek world through the ministry of the disciples, many of whom are Jews and gentiles.

Jesus now states for the first time that his hour has come. It is the hour for glorification that includes Jesus' obedience to God's will, even to the point of death. The meaning of Jesus' hour is shown through the image of a grain of wheat that can bear no fruit unless it falls to the earth and dies. Otherwise, the grain has no use and remains a mere grain of wheat. Just as the grain of wheat that falls to the ground and dies bears much fruit, so Jesus, by his death and resurrection, will bring forth a rich harvest for eternal life. Jesus calls his disciples to this same mission. Those who live only to preserve their earthly life will lose eternal salvation, while those who are willing to sacrifice in this life will gain eternal life. Jesus invites those who wish to follow him to share in his hour and follow him as true servants, promising the Father's reward.

Though John presents Jesus as a divine king, he also stresses Christ's humanity by showing Jesus' fear in the face of his passion and death. Despite his fear, Jesus does not ask the Father to spare him from his hour, since he realizes that this hour is central to his mission and for the glory of the Father. In response to Jesus' acceptance of his mission, a voice cries out from heaven that God's name has been glorified and will continue to be glorified. When the crowd hears the voice, some declare that it is thunder, while others believe an angel has spoken. Jesus proclaims, "This voice did not come for my sake, but for yours" (12:30). The crowd now learns that Jesus, by accepting his "hour" (the time of his passion, death, resurrection, and ascension) will defeat the ruler of the world, namely the power of evil.

John repeats the message that Jesus will be lifted up. Although this implies the exaltation of Jesus in his resurrection, the author informs us that he is speaking about the death of Jesus on the cross. The crowd challenges Jesus' words, stating that the Messiah is to remain forever. When Jesus states that the Son of Man must be lifted up, the crowd asks who this Son of Man is. Jesus does not answer their question directly but speaks of himself as the light who has come into the world. He informs them that the light will be among them only a little while longer. In a short time, the hour of darkness will arrive, and those who walk in the darkness of evil will be spiritually lost. Jesus is present to them now, but his crucifixion will be a time of darkness and a time when many will turn against him. Those who follow the light (Jesus) will continue to believe and will be called the children of light. Jesus then departs from the crowds and goes into hiding.

Lectio Divina

Spend 8 to 10 minutes in silent contemplation of the following passage:

Jesus viewed himself as a grain of wheat that must die in order to produce fruit. He feared his form of death, but he was willing to accept it to bring glory to God. Courage and love are not shown through a lack of fear, but through acting despite fear. He was willing to be lifted up on the cross for our salvation. We are meant to be like the grain of wheat that must die in some manner to produce fruit. Just as Christ was lifted up, we too are lifted up, not on a cross, but as a known Christian. Our manner of life can show us to be people who live in the light by following Jesus, or people who live in darkness by rejecting Christ.

✠ *What can I learn from this passage?*

Day 5: Belief and Unbelief Among the Jews (12:37–50)

John tells us that the crowd refuses to believe in Jesus, despite the many signs he has performed in their midst, and he quotes from the prophet Isaiah (Isaiah 53:1), who had already foretold this rejection. As a motive for it, the author adds another quote from Isaiah asserting that God blinded their eyes and hardened their heart so that they would not see and understand (Isaiah 6:9). Only an open heart is capable of understanding the message of Christ.

Because of Isaiah's recognition of God's work in the world, he could claim to have seen Jesus' glory. John adds that some among the religious leaders believed in him, but they remained silent, fearing they would be thrown out of the synagogue. This most likely applied to the religious leaders who lived in the early Church era, when those who professed faith in Jesus were cast out of the Temple. During Jesus' lifetime, his disciples were not cast out of the synagogues. John notes that those who kept their belief in Jesus secret loved human glory instead of God's.

Jesus summarizes lessons he already taught. He repeats his claim that those who believe in him and look on him with faith will see the one who sent him. He comes into the world as the Light of the World to free those who believe in him from living in darkness, "not come to condemn the world, but to save it." Those who reject him become their own judge, for they are rejecting the message he has given. Jesus' words will condemn them. The Son has been faithful to the Father's message. Finally, Jesus proclaims that the Father wills eternal life. In this summary, Jesus reiterates both his role as the Light of the World and as the one sent by the Father.

Lectio Divina

Spend 8 to 10 minutes in silent contemplation of the following passage:

Jesus repeats his message that he is the Light of the World and one with God the Father. Those who believe in Jesus must proclaim their faith openly so that the light of Christ can be seen through their lives. Since Jesus left a new command of love for the world, it is no longer necessary for Jesus to condemn anyone, since his teachings have already condemned those who hear them and refuse to follow them. Jesus did not come to condemn anyone, but rather to bring salvation to the world.

✠ *What can I learn from this passage?*

Review Questions

1. Why were Caiaphas' words ironic when he called for the killing of Jesus?
2. What is significant about Jesus' anointing in Bethany?
3. Why is Jesus' glorious entry into Jerusalem so important?
4. What does Jesus mean when he uses the image of the grain of wheat that must die to produce fruit?

Jesus Sends an Advocate

JOHN 13:1–16:33

Do not let your hearts be troubled. You have faith in God; have faith also in me. In my Father's house there are many dwelling places. If there were not, would I have told you that I am going to prepare a place for you? (14:1–2).

Opening Prayer (SEE PAGE 18)

Context

Part 1: John 13:1—14:14 Jesus washes his disciples' feet at the Last Supper, setting an example of humility and helping them to understand what they must do for others. Here, Christ issues a new commandment, to love one another. He tells the disciples that he will be leaving them soon to be with the Father.

Part 2: John 14:15—16:33 Jesus promises to send an Advocate, the Spirit of truth. The Advocate, whom the Father will send in Jesus' name, will teach them everything and remind them of all that Jesus told them. Jesus commands the disciples once again to love one another, addressing his followers as friends. Though the Lord instructs that the disciples will be hated by the world, he tells his followers not to fear for the Spirit will be their guide.

PART 1: GROUP STUDY (JOHN 13:1—14:14)

Read aloud John 13:1—14:14.

13:1–20 Jesus washes the feet of his disciples

The Book of Glory begins with the Last Supper, containing the final discourses of Jesus. Although the whole Gospel of John slowly reveals the glory of the Son of God as related to the glory of the Father, this section moves Jesus through his passion and death to his resurrection. This book contains lengthy discourses and prayers for Jesus' disciples and all believers.

At the Last Supper, John again stresses that the Passover is near. Unlike the synoptic Gospels, he makes no mention of the details during the supper, or of the eucharistic aspects of the meal. The hour of Jesus' glorification has arrived, and it will begin with his passing from this world to the Father. This passing becomes the new Passover. Death is not presented as a failure because it concludes with a passage to the Father, which is truly a passage to glory.

Judas, under the influence of the evil one, has already decided to betray Jesus. John portrays Jesus as one who is well aware that he comes from God and will thus return to God; like the prophets of old who at times acted out their prophecies, Jesus, by washing the feet of his disciples and drying them with a towel, plays the role of a servant and instructs his disciples that they must do the same. In Jesus' day, it was the ordinary task of a slave to wash the feet of visitors at a banquet; but here the Lord becomes the example for all disciples. The Lord's example calls all disciples to serve.

Just as Peter attempted to reject Jesus' prediction of his death and resurrection in the synoptic Gospels, in John's Gospel he tries to thwart Jesus' attempt to wash his feet. Throughout the gospels, Peter seems uncomfortable with the servant image of Jesus. Only later will Peter be able to understand the full meaning of Jesus' actions. When Peter objects, Jesus tells him that he (Peter) will have no part of him (Jesus) unless he accepts this washing. Peter, true to character, goes to extremes and offers his hands and head for the washing, illustrating his desire and enthusiasm to share in Christ's life. Jesus tells him there is no need for this as long as one has been made clean in the bathing of the feet. Because Jesus knows his betrayer, he informs his disciples that not all of them are clean. Having finished the action of washing the disciples' feet, Jesus now draws a lesson from his action.

Jesus reminds his disciples that they too are aware of his high position, rightly calling him "Teacher" and "Lord." Just as he is willing to humble himself as a servant in washing their feet, so they, following his example, should offer themselves as servants for the sake of others. They can easily accept the argument that no servant and no messenger is greater than one's master. If Jesus, as master, is willing to act in this fashion, then his disciples should do the same. Once they accept this teaching and act accordingly, they will share in God's blessings. Jesus' continual message to his disciples in all the gospels is that they should serve others as he did.

13:21–30 Announcement of Judas' betrayal

In John's Gospel, Jesus is fully aware of the strengths and weaknesses of those he has chosen, and, although saddened, he is not surprised at Judas' betrayal. To show that God has complete control of the world, we are told by Jesus through the gospel writer that his purpose in choosing these men was the fulfillment of the Scriptures. This has led to many questions concerning the free will of Judas, most notably whether he had a choice in betraying Jesus. John makes no attempt to settle this issue here but simply wishes to acknowledge that the hour of darkness has come, and those who live in darkness will have their moment of power.

Jesus quotes from Psalm 41:9, which states that the one who partook of the meal was the one to betray him. To the Jews, sharing a meal signified sharing in one's life; therefore, the seriousness of Judas' betrayal is shown more forcefully as he rejects a life he once shared. Jesus tells his disciples that he is now predicting this betrayal, so that when it occurs they will not lose faith but will remember him as "I AM." Those who accept Christ accept the one who sent him, but not all will accept him. Jesus is disturbed when he announces that one of them will betray him. This causes some uneasiness among the disciples, and Peter signals the one closest to Jesus, the one whom Jesus loved, to ask who the betrayer is. Jesus answers that it is the one to whom he gives a piece of food dipped in the dish. This is a sign of sharing and of honor for the person chosen to receive his morsel.

Some see this as Jesus' attempt to lure Judas back into his graces, which would reflect God's untiring desire to seek the return to grace of all sinners.

Judas rejects the invitation to repent, and the power of evil overtakes him. Jesus tells him to perform his duties quickly, and the others believe that Jesus is sending him on an errand as the treasurer of the group. Judas leaves, and the author tells us in a short and stark sentence, "And it was night." The power of darkness is now at work.

13:31–38 The new commandment

As Judas departs, Jesus launches into a lengthy farewell discourse. The author develops this discourse, as he has done throughout his gospel, with questions placed at specific points that help Jesus deliver his message. Because Jesus has already stated that he and the Father are one, he can now declare that the moment of his glorification is about to take place, and with it, glory will be given to the Father. He will not be physically with them much longer, and he tells them they will not go with him because they still have their mission to perform. He leaves them with a new commandment to love one another. The commandment itself is not new, but the model of that love, namely, Jesus' love for his disciples, is new. They must love others as Jesus has loved them. If they love as Jesus loved, the world will recognize them as his disciples.

A tradition found in all the gospels is Peter's brave intent to follow Jesus to death and his weak response at the time of Jesus' trial. John records Peter's bold statement that he will lay down his life for Christ. Jesus predicts that Peter will deny him three times before the cock crows. The early readers of this gospel were most likely aware that Peter, who was martyred for Christ in Rome around 64, did eventually lay down his life for Christ.

14:1—14:14 Last Supper discourses

Jesus tells his disciples not to let their hearts be troubled. With all that has been happening on this evening, the disciples have every reason to be disturbed. Jesus urges them to remain calm and to place their faith in God and in him. Although they know the events that will take place in Jesus' life, Jesus is telling them that they should also view the spiritual consequences of those events.

Jesus teaches that there are many dwelling places in "my Father's house." Heaven was seen by the Jews as God's Temple and dwelling place. God has room for everyone; otherwise Jesus' mission would have been in vain. Jesus now prepares a place for them by going before them into God's dwelling place. After Jesus has passed to the Father through his death, resurrection, and ascension, he will return to take his disciples with him. These words of Jesus prompt a response from Thomas, who states that they do not know where Jesus is going, much less how to get to this place. Because Jesus is going to the Father, the emphasis should not be put on the place, but on the person of the Father. If the disciples really know Jesus, they will also know the Father to whom he is going. The way to the Father is through Jesus, who proclaims that he is the way, the truth, and the life.

Despite the time Jesus has spent with his disciples, they still do not fully understand his message. All four gospels show that the followers of Jesus did not fully grasp the meaning of his life until after the resurrection. Philip, anxious to learn more, urges Jesus to show them the Father. Jesus, sounding somewhat frustrated, tells Philip that he has been with them for so long, and they still do not know him. Philip's question becomes the springboard for Jesus to continue teaching his message.

Jesus and the Father are one, and the words of Jesus are the words of the Father. Those who have faith in Jesus should be able to accept this union of Father and Son. If they cannot, then Jesus urges them to accept him because of his works, which are those of the Father. Jesus states that those who have faith will perform works so great as to be likened to Christ's signs and wonders; in fact, according to the Lord, they will perform even greater works. This will happen because Jesus, who is going to the Father, will answer their requests and bring glory to the Father. Throughout the gospel, Jesus emphasized that the glory given to the Son is also magnifying the Father's majesty.

Review Questions

1. How can we apply Jesus' act of washing the feet of his disciples to our lives?

2. Why were Jesus' disciples unable to recognize Judas as Jesus' betrayer after Jesus identified him by handing him a morsel that he had dipped in the bowl?

3. Why does Jesus' new commandment to love one another challenge us? Explain.

4. Discuss Jesus' claim that those who see him see the Father. What is significant about this claim? What does this teach us about Jesus? The Father?

Closing Prayer (SEE PAGE 18)

Pray the closing prayer now or after *lectio divina*.

Lectio Divina (SEE PAGE 11)

Relax your body and maintain a posture of prayer (back straight, eyes shut, feet flat on the floor). This exercise can take as long as you want, but in the context of this Bible study, 10 to 20 minutes should be sufficient.

The meditations that follow are provided only to help group participants use this prayer form, but note that *lectio* is intended to bring one to a place of prayerful contemplation where the Word of God speaks to the hearer from his or her heart. See page 11 for further instruction.

Jesus washes the feet of his disciples (13:1–20)

Jesus gives us an example of servant discipleship as he himself washes the feet of his disciples at the Last Supper. Although he does not change the bread and wine into his Body and Blood in John's Gospel, he teaches a message about Eucharist when he washes the disciple's feet. He is telling us that we are a eucharistic people, and as such, we are called to serve with humility. Service is at the center of Eucharist, and Jesus serves us by giving us his Body and Blood; we serve by humbly serving others as Jesus served his disciples. If God can take a position of humility and servanthood, then true followers of Christ must do the same.

✠ *What can I learn from this passage?*

Announcement of Judas' betrayal (13:21–30)

In Psalm 55, we can glimpse some of Jesus' grief due to Judas' betrayal. The psalmist writes: "For it is not an enemy that reviled me—that I could bear—Not a foe who viewed me with contempt, from that I could hide. But it was you, my other self, my comrade and friend, you, whose company I enjoyed, at whose side I walked in the house of God" (Psalm 55:13–15). Jesus, the Light of the World, would be challenged by the darkness of grief at this moment, but darkness as crushing as the betrayal by a friend like Judas cannot overcome the Light of the World.

✠ *What can I learn from this passage?*

The new commandment (13:31–38)

Not only are we called to love one another, likewise we are called to love others as Jesus loves us. Peter offers us a brief example of love and weakness. He brags that he will lay down his life for Jesus, but manages to fail at first. Later, however, Peter will offer his life for Christ. His weakness during Jesus' passion teaches us that the call to love as Jesus loved may take time and involve a number of failures. As disciples of Jesus, we must continue to reach out for the goal of loving as Jesus loved.

✠ *What can I learn from this passage?*

Last Supper discourses (14:1–14)

Jesus tells his disciples not to let their hearts be troubled. As followers of Jesus, we know that we can trust that Jesus is with us in every challenge of our life. This thought fills us with hope and lessens our anxiety. Jesus also states that in his Father's house, there are many dwelling places. There are many different forms of spirituality that lead to sainthood. That is God's will for all of us.

In the desert, Saint Anthony practiced a spirituality that differed from that of Saint Ignatius; and Saint Ignatius practiced a spirituality other than that of Saint Francis of Assisi. Our call is to perform our duties in life as well as possible and to strive to love others as Jesus loves us. With the help of spiritual reading or a spiritual director, we are meant to discern our own form of spirituality; a sincere desire to love God and others as Jesus loved.

✠ *What can I learn from this passage?*

PART 2: INDIVIDUAL STUDY (JOHN 14:15—16:33)

Day 1: The Advocate (14:15–31)

Those who love Jesus are faithful to his commands. These commands were given not only in words, but also by the example of Jesus found throughout the gospel. Promising not to leave his disciples orphaned, Jesus tells them that he will send another Advocate who will be with them always. Jesus himself is the Advocate from the Father, and he promises to send the Holy Spirit, another Advocate. This Advocate will be sent by the Son and the Father and will be recognized only by those who live a life of faith, not by those who live for the flesh alone. Through this Advocate, Jesus will return to his disciples.

Jesus tells his disciples that very soon they will no longer see him, but he then adds that they will see him as the one who shares life with them. The word "see" has two different connotations here. The disciples will no longer see the physical Jesus with their human eyes, but they will see, or perceive, the presence of the divine Son through the eyes of faith. When this happens, they will understand that Jesus and the Father are one. Those who love and believe in Jesus will be loved by the Father, Son, and Spirit, and Jesus will reveal himself to them through faith.

In the Gospel of Luke, Jesus chooses two men named Judas as members of the Twelve (Luke 6:16). John tells us that Judas, not the Iscariot, asks Jesus why he is revealing himself only to them and not to the world. This question enables the author to continue Jesus' discourse. Jesus tells Judas that those who are open to loving him will be faithful to his message, and that he and the Father will come to dwell with them. Those who do not love him will not keep his word, and this hinders the Father and the Son from dwelling within such people. The message the believers accept does not come from Christ alone but from the Father. The mission of the Advocate, the Holy Spirit, is to open our minds to Jesus' teachings.

On his departure, Jesus wishes his followers the customary "Peace." But the peace he leaves with them is deeper; it comes from Jesus and is a life-giving peace. Because Jesus is going to the Father, the disciples should rejoice rather than grieve. Jesus states that the Father is greater than he.

This should not be taken to mean that the Father and Son are not equal; rather, that during Jesus' earthly life, he was limited his human condition with all its weaknesses. Because of these limitations, the Father guided Jesus' footsteps in order to show us the way to God.

Jesus is speaking about the end in this way so that the faith of his disciples will not be shattered when he dies. In the resurrection of Jesus, they will recall his words and be ready to understand with the eyes of faith. The present moment, however, belongs to the prince of darkness. Jesus is not undergoing this hour of darkness because evil has control over him but because of his love for and obedience to the Father. Jesus ends this discourse abruptly as he sets out to face his hour with the words of one sent on a final and urgent mission: "Rise up, let us go."

Lectio Divina

Spend 8 to 10 minutes in silent contemplation of the following passage:

> Jesus says at the end of his passage, "Rise up, let us go." Linking these words with the passage, we can say that Jesus sent us the Holy Spirit so that the world will perceive that Christ is with us. The experience of God's presence in us can only be known through the gift of the Advocate who comes from the Father and the Son. The Advocate will inspire us to love God, who loves us deeply and infinitely. With the coming of the Advocate, God will dwell within us. Our ministry is to share Christ's message with those around us. "Get up, let us go."

✠ *What can I learn from this passage?*

Day 2: The Vine and the Branches (15:1–17)

After telling us at the end of the last chapter that Jesus decides to move on from the place of his last discourse ("Rise up, let us go"), the author has Jesus begin a new and much longer discourse, which repeats in more detail the message given in chapter fourteen. In a later chapter (18:1), Jesus and his disciples move across the Kidron Valley, a journey that would more obviously follow chapter fourteen. Many commentators suspect that this longer discourse in John 15 is an addition made during one of the earliest editions of this gospel.

The image of God planting a vineyard in Israel is often used in Old Testament writings. Isaiah writes about a vineyard planted by God that produces only sour grapes. The vineyard is God's Chosen People and the sour grapes refer to the sins of the people. Isaiah warns that God will destroy the hedges surrounding the vineyard, leaving it open to grazing and destruction. The inhabitants of Jerusalem will soon experience a horrible slaughter and exile at the hands of the Babylonians (Isaiah 5:1–7).

Although the vineyard in the Old Testament is often connoted as Israel, Jesus uses the image to speak of the vine and the vine grower. He is the vine, and his Father is the vine grower, the one who cares for the vine and sees to its growth. Like the busy vine grower, the Father will prune away every barren branch (false disciple), and will trim the good branches (the good disciples) so that they can yield more fruit. Jesus tells his disciples that because of the words they have received from him, they are the fruitful branches. Jesus is sharing his message with his disciples, the new Chosen People of God. The First Letter of Peter addressing the baptized followers of Jesus after the resurrection proclaims: "But you are 'a chosen race, a royal priesthood, a holy nation, a people of his own, so that you may announce the praises' of him who called you out of darkness into his wonderful light" (1 Peter 2:9).

The yield of the disciples will depend on their remaining in Christ, the vine. Just as the branches live in the vine and the vine lives in the branches, so they live in Jesus and Jesus lives in them. Cut off from Christ, they are useless and destined to be burned. As a branch linked to the vine, they receive the life they need from Jesus, and they will have their requests granted. As true disciples, they will not only bring glory to Christ in their abundant harvest, but they will also bring glory to the Father.

After Jesus speaks of the unity between himself and the disciples, he names the life-giving source of that union—love. The love that the Son receives from the Father is shared with his disciples, who are urged to live in that love. Jesus offers himself as a model. Just as he lives in the Father's love by keeping the Father's commandments, so they are to live in Jesus' love by keeping his commandments. The message Jesus gives them is one of true spiritual joy where they will find complete fulfillment. In summary, Jesus urges them to follow his commandment to love one another.

Jesus tells his disciples the extent of his love for them. He will lay down his life for them, the greatest sign of one's love for a friend. Although Jesus shared in the creation of the world and was with the Father from all eternity, he does not consider his disciples to be slaves, but he calls them friends. Keeping in mind the high image of Jesus Christ presented in his gospel, the author is sharing an overwhelming message with his readers at this point. As friends who keep the commandments of Jesus, the disciples share the secrets passed on to them from the Father through Jesus.

Jesus tells his disciples that they did not choose him, but he chose them. They now have the duty of sharing the message with the world as Christ shared it with them. This message will bear abundant fruit, and all they ask of the Father will be granted to them. The message is not just one of words, but it is the fulfillment of Christ's command to love one another.

Lectio Divina

Spend 8 to 10 minutes in silent contemplation of the following passage:

> Jesus is the vine, the giver of life, and we are the branches. As long as we live a life faithful to Christ, we will bear much fruit—an example of Christ's love. Jesus no longer views us as servants of his message but as friends who share his joy because we believe that he and the Father are one. Jesus' message of friendship is shown as he declares that there is no greater sign of love for a friend than to lay down one's life. Jesus laid down his life for us, and he calls us to lay down our lives in return. In this way, Jesus is the vine, and we are the branches.

> ✠ *What can I learn from this passage?*

Day 3: The World's Hatred (15:18—16:4)

Jesus says, "If the world hates you, realize that it hated me first" (15:18). When Jesus speaks of the world in this section, he is speaking of the material world that judges everything from its own earthly perspective. It is the world of darkness and sin, a world that rejects Jesus—the image of God's love. The disciples should not be surprised that the world hates them, since it first hated Jesus. The sad part of Jesus' message is that the world will reject the disciples because they speak in the name of Jesus. If Jesus had not given these others a chance to change their lives, they would not be guilty of sin in rejecting him and the Father. Just as the one who loves Christ loves the Father, so the one who hates Christ hates the Father. Jesus not only taught the disciples about himself and the Father, but he also performed signs that pointed to the truth of this message. If he had not performed these works among them, they would not be guilty of sin. Despite what they have seen, they continue in their rejection; in doing so, they fulfill an Old Testament prophecy from Psalm 69:5: "they hated me without cause."

Jesus speaks again of the Advocate who will come to them. In the previous chapter, he spoke of the ministry of the Holy Spirit as one of instruction. He now addresses the Spirit as the Spirit of truth and thus the ministry of the Advocate to witness. The Holy Spirit will witness on behalf of the truth, and the disciples, who have been with Jesus since his ministry began, must join in this witnessing. The author, at the time of the writing of the gospel, knows that Christians are already facing expulsion from the synagogues and persecution for their faith in Jesus, and he reminds them that these events were foreseen by Jesus. Those responsible for casting them out of synagogues and putting them to death never knew Jesus or the Father. The words of Jesus are meant to sustain their faith at this fateful hour.

Lectio Divina

Spend 8 to 10 minutes in silent contemplation of the following passage:

> The number of Christian martyrs in the world today confirm Jesus' message that his disciples should not be surprised if the world hates them as they hated our Lord. Christians who follow Jesus' law of love do not perform any actions intended to hurt others, but they become victims despite the good they seek to do. Jesus is instructing us that we should not be surprised if people reject us because we live and act with a loving concern for others. The Advocate will fill us with faith in Jesus, and we have the duty of testifying to Jesus, even if those whose lives center only on the world reject us. Jesus

warns us that we may be rejected for our faith so that we should not be surprised if we encounter opposition by others.

✠ *What can I learn from this passage?*

Day 4: The Coming of the Spirit (16:4b–24)

As long as Jesus remained with his disciples, he had no need to speak to them at length about the Holy Spirit. Now that his death draws near and he is about to return to the Father, he gives a more lengthy discourse on the activity of the Holy Spirit. Although Jesus begins by telling his disciples that none of them is asking where he is going, the fact is that Peter (13:36) and Thomas (14:5) have both asked that very question. Some commentators see this as a sign that chapter sixteen does not belong to the earliest manuscript of this gospel.

Jesus recognizes the grief of his disciples, but he tells them that they should be rejoicing rather than lamenting. Jesus must go in order for the Holy Spirit to come to them, who himself will send the Advocate upon them. In turn, the Spirit will help the disciples understand God's plan and interpret the events of Jesus' life. The Holy Spirit will enlighten the hearts of believers and help them understand the mysteries of God.

The Advocate will continue to teach the disciples the message Jesus wishes to share with them. The Spirit will guide them, and Jesus will speak through the "Spirit of truth." In speaking the message received from Jesus, the Spirit gives glory to him. Just as the Father gives all he has to the Son, so the Son gives all he has to the Spirit. Jesus ends this part of his discourse by announcing that the disciples will not see him for a short time, but that they will see him again soon. This reference may be to the death and resurrection of Jesus, or, more likely, to the presence of him in the gift of the Holy Spirit.

Jesus' words, "a little while," draw the disciples back into the conversation. They question among themselves the meaning of these words. Jesus, aware of their desire to question him, indirectly answers their question by telling them that their pain will be similar to that of a woman in labor. Just as a woman who has passed through the pain of childbirth will forget her pain when the child is born, so the disciples will go through grief and pain but will rejoice when Jesus comes to them again. The reference is to Jesus' resurrection, but in order to understand this mystery the Spirit must enlighten them. Although Jesus will not be with them in the way he was during his earthly life, they will know his presence whenever they ask the Father in Jesus' name for whatever they want.

Lectio Divina

Spend 8 to 10 minutes in silent contemplation of the following passage:

Jesus, recognizing our need for the Advocate (the Holy Spirit) in understanding his message, promises to send us the Spirit after his death and resurrection. His death will bring grief to his disciples, but it will also bring a great reward, namely the gift of the Holy Spirit upon the world. The Holy Spirit will bring glory to Jesus because the Spirit will give us a greater understanding of Jesus' message. The disciples of Jesus will grieve, but the pain of grief will give way to joy when they realize the great gift of resurrection and ascension. Through the gift of the Holy Spirit, we will pray with faith to God in the name of Jesus. The life of Jesus continues in the world through God's gift of the Holy Spirit.

✠ *What can I learn from this passage?*

Day 5: Jesus Departure (16:25–33)

Until now, Jesus has spoken to his disciples in veiled language concerning the Father, but the time is coming when he will speak to them more clearly. The language of Jesus concerning the Father is confusing for the disciples. They will not be capable of recognizing the full meaning of Jesus' ministry until after his death and resurrection. The Father will respond to the prayers they pray in Jesus' name, not because Jesus intercedes for them, but because the Father honors the name of the Son. The Father, who loves the Son, also loves the disciples who love Jesus and have faith in him.

The disciples, in a moment of enthusiasm, declare they now understand all that Jesus, who knows all things, has taught them. They bravely proclaim they believe that Jesus came from God. Jesus chides them, asking if they really believe. He warns that the hour has already come when they will be scattered, leaving him alone. Despite their claims of understanding Jesus, they will abandon him during his passion and death, but Christ declares he is never truly alone, because the Father is always present with him. In the final warning of this chapter, Jesus tells the disciples they will indeed suffer, but they will also find peace in him who has overcome the power of evil in the world.

Lectio Divina

Spend 8 to 10 minutes in silent contemplation of the following passage:

The conflict in the hearts of the disciples can be likened to our own struggle. We believe that Jesus is the Christ, the Son of God. Jesus tells us to love one another and love our enemies, but remaining faithful to Jesus' message is difficult. When we are faced with conflict, the real challenge of being a follower of Christ becomes dominant. How different are we from the disciples? As we struggle with our desire to be faithful to Christ in those difficult moments of conflict, we can easily understand why the disciples would flee. The saving grace in being a follower of Jesus is that Jesus loves us, understands our weakness, and will invite us to try again.

✠ *What can I learn from this passage?*

Review Questions

1. What does Jesus mean when he says that he will not leave his disciples orphaned?
2. Why is the Advocate important in our life?
3. Explain the significance of Jesus' teaching about the vine and the branches.
4. Why should Jesus' disciples expect to encounter rejection in the world?

The Crucifixion of Jesus

JOHN 17:1—19:42

So they took Jesus, and carrying the cross himself he went out to what is called the Place of the Skull, in Hebrew, Golgotha. There they crucified him, and with him two others, one on either side, with Jesus in the middle (John 19:16b–18).

Opening Prayer (SEE PAGE 18)

Context

Part 1: John 17:1—18:14 Here we listen to Jesus pray for the protection of his disciples and for all those who do not yet belong to the Father. Afterward, the passion narrative begins with the arrest of Jesus and betrayal of Judas Iscariot.

Part 2: John 18:15—19:42 Jesus is condemned to death by Pontius Pilate at the insistence of the crowd, though he found Jesus to be without guilt. Christ is then scourged, ridiculed, and crucified. Blood and water flow out of Jesus' side when he is pierced with a spear after his death. Joseph of Arimathea and Nicodemus bury Jesus, having asked Pontius Pilate for his body.

Part 1: Group Study (John 17:1—18:14)

Read aloud John 17:1—18:14.

17:1—17:26 Jesus' priestly prayer for his disciples

Many commentators refer to Jesus' words in this chapter as the "High Priestly Prayer" of Jesus. Jesus looks up to heaven, a common posture for prayer, and prays directly to the Father. He again proclaims that the hour has come for the Father to give glory to the Son so that the Son may give glory to the Father. In this prayer, Jesus is conscious of those in the world who serve him, and he expresses his desire to bestow eternal life on them.

The central theme of these verses tells us that eternal life consists in knowing with an active faith the only true God and Jesus Christ, the one sent by the Father. This "knowing" is not just an intellectual faith but one that deeply touches a person's life. Now that the hour has come, Jesus can declare that he has fulfilled the mission given to him by the Father. He prays that the Father will give him the place of glory that he had from the beginning. The Son, who existed with the Father before the beginning of the world, is returning to his place of glory with the Father.

Addressing the Father, Jesus states that the disciples have accepted his Word, the Father's Word. Although the disciples did not fully understand the meaning of Jesus' life and message until after the resurrection, Jesus commends them for their faith by believing that Jesus was sent by the Father. Although Jesus is concerned for all people of the world, he expressly states that his prayer at this time is only for his disciples. In John's Gospel, discipleship is important; the disciples of Jesus will be the ones "sent" when the Advocate comes. Just as everything that belongs to the Son also belongs to the Father, so Jesus' disciples belong to the Father. After the resurrection, the disciples will be the ones who remain in the world and bring glory to God.

Jesus prays that the Father will protect the disciples and unify them by the Son, who illumines the Father. He claims that he has protected them while he was with them, although he admits that he was not able to protect the betrayer who was destined to be lost. The author of the gospel, writing after the events of Jesus' passion and death, realized that Judas had betrayed Jesus. John is not stating that Judas had no choice in betraying Jesus, but that Judas was the one whom God had foreseen as the betrayer.

As he stated in an earlier chapter, Jesus tells his disciples all this so they will not be confused when his passion and death take place. Not only will Jesus suffer, but they too will suffer because they will be living with faith in Jesus' words. Just as Christ does not belong to the ways of the world and will be rejected by it, so the disciples too can expect to be scoffed at in the same way. Jesus prays that the Father will protect the disciples and consecrate them by means of truth. It is this dedication to truth that will lead Jesus to his death and resurrection, a path that the disciples also must trod.

Jesus now turns his attention to all of his followers, including those of the future. His central prayer for them is that they will be one with God and with one another, just as he and the Father are one. This example of unity will be a sign to the world that they are sent by God, and, through it, the world will recognize God's love for them. Jesus prays that his disciples will remain with him and will witness the glory given to him by the Father because of the love the Father has had for him before the beginning of time. Jesus states in his prayer that he, not the world, knows the Father, and that he shares this knowledge with those who believe. He will continue to share this knowledge of the Father with future disciples so that the love of the Father that resides in the Son will also live in his disciples through his life poured out on them.

18:1–14 Jesus is arrested

The passion narrative begins with Jesus' arrest, and except for several omissions and a few additions, the writer follows the description of the passion found in the synoptic Gospels. Jesus goes out with his disciples across the Kidron Valley, a small valley between the Mount of Olives and Jerusalem. John has already mentioned that Jesus made several visits to Jerusalem. Although John does not name the garden where Jesus and his disciples meet, it is safe to conclude that it is the Garden of Olives named in the synoptic Gospels. We can presume that on each trip to Jerusalem, they stayed at the same spot in the Garden of Olives. This would explain how Judas knew where to find Jesus. Judas and those sent by the chief priests and the Pharisees came with lanterns, torches, and weapons, emphasizing the movement of evil in the midst of darkness.

Jesus asks who they want, and they reply that they are looking for Jesus of Nazareth. Jesus tells them, "I AM," and they fall to the ground in the presence of the true God. Jesus again asks whom they are seeking, and they answer, as before, that they are seeking Jesus of Nazareth. In offering himself, Jesus asks that the crowd allow his disciples to go free. John sees this as a fulfillment of Jesus' proclamation that he would not lose any of those given to him by the Father. The scene also shows Jesus' complete control of the situation. In John's Gospel, Jesus continues to control the events of the passion. John omits Jesus' agony in the garden, perhaps to avoid any image of Jesus' weak human condition. John is concerned more with the solid, divine image of Jesus.

Peter steps forward and with his sword cuts off the right ear of Malchus, the high priest's servant. Although the synoptic Gospels mention this incident, only John names Peter as the one who wields the sword and Malchus as the servant whose ear is cut off. By telling Peter to put his sword back into its place, Jesus states his willingness to accept the cup given him by the Father. This cup is a cup of suffering, and it is mentioned in the synoptic Gospels during Jesus' agony in the garden. The soldiers arrest Jesus, bind him, and lead him to Annas, the father-in-law of the high priest Caiaphas. The author reminds us that it was Caiaphas who said that it was fitting for one man to die for the people.

Review Questions

1. Why did Jesus feel a need to pray for his disciples?
2. Why is unity among Christians important to Jesus? How does Christ unify our communities? Give some examples.
3. What is the significance of Jesus saying "I AM" when he is arrested?
4. Discuss the events that took place during the arrest of Jesus.

Closing Prayer (SEE PAGE 18)

Pray the closing prayer now or after *lectio divina*.

Lectio Divina (SEE PAGE 11)

Relax your body and maintain a posture of prayer (back straight, eyes shut, feet flat on the floor). This exercise can take as long as you want, but in the context of this Bible study, 10 to 20 minutes should be sufficient.

The meditations that follow are provided only to help group participants use this prayer form, but note that *lectio* is intended to bring one to a place of prayerful contemplation where the Word of God speaks to the hearer from his or her heart. See page 11 for further instruction.

Jesus' priestly prayer for his disciples (17:1–26)

Jesus prays for his disciples, asking the Father's blessings on those the Father gives him. He prays that they will glorify him and be consecrated to the truth. Although Jesus apparently prayed for the disciples of his own day, he also prayed for us as we live our faith in unity with him. Just as the Father sent Jesus into the world, so Jesus sends us to share his message. We serve as disciples who share in Jesus' prayer.

✠ *What can I learn from this passage?*

Jesus is arrested (18:1–14)

As the passion narrative begins, Jesus shows his usual concern for his disciples. He requests that those arresting him allow his disciples to go. Joseph Cardinal Bernardin of Chicago is one who offers an example of a true disciple of Jesus. When he was dying of cancer, he began visiting cancer victims. He claimed that before he did this, he was thinking of himself and his own sickness, but once he began to visit those dying of the dreaded disease, he found himself thinking less of himself and more of others. When we are sick or have personal struggles, we tend to spend most of our time thinking about ourselves and our own suffering, but Jesus reaches out and challenges us to follow his example.

✠ *What can I learn from this passage?*

PART 2: INDIVIDUAL STUDY (JOHN 18:15—19:42)

Day 1: Peter's Denials (18:15–27)

As Jesus is led off, Peter and another disciple follow behind the crowd. Because this other disciple is known to those in the courtyard of the high priest, he is able to gain entrance for himself and Peter. Some commentators believe that this "other disciple" may be the "beloved disciple" who was at the foot of the cross with the Mother of Jesus when Jesus was crucified. The servant girl who tends the gate questions Peter, asking if he is not indeed one of Jesus' followers. Peter replies, "I am not," and goes to warm himself by the fire. At the same time Peter utters his first cowardly denial, Jesus is standing courageously before Annas.

When the accusers ask Jesus about his disciples and his message, he answers that he had preached openly in the synagogues and the Temple to any who would listen to him. He had nothing to hide from anyone but suggests that they question those who heard him who will be able to tell the leaders what he preached. One of the guards slaps Jesus, asking him if this is any way to speak to the high priest. Though Annas is not the high priest, he is a powerful figure in Jerusalem and one who held the position for almost seven years. Likewise he had five sons as well as his son-in-law named high priest in the years after him. Jesus, knowing his rights, challenges the guards to show cause for striking him. Annas sends Jesus, who is still bound, to Caiaphas, whom the author again names as the high priest.

Jesus' courageous stand before the high priest is sandwiched between Peter's denials. Those standing around the fire with Peter ask if he is a disciple of Jesus, and he denies it. A relative of the one whose ear he had cut off questions whether Peter was in the garden, and Peter denies this. As Jesus had predicted, the cock begins to crow after this last denial. John makes no mention of Peter's reaction.

Lectio Divina

Spend 8 to 10 minutes in silent contemplation of the following passage:

The passion of Jesus now becomes a passion for Peter, who must watch his close friend die after denying him, a friend he had come to believe was the Christ. After Jesus' resurrection, we meet the new Peter, one who is truly ready to die for Jesus, and eventually does. In our lives, we may be weak and deny Christ in some way, but Peter shows us that no matter how far we fall, we can still become a staunch and faithful follower of Jesus. Peter teaches us that it is never too late to turn back to Christ and become a totally dedicated disciple.

✠ *What can I learn from this passage?*

Day 2: The Trial Before Pilate (18:28–40)

Although Jesus is brought to Caiaphas, John gives no details about the confrontation between Jesus and the high priest. At daybreak, the Jewish leaders bring Jesus to the headquarters of the Roman court where Pilate, the procurator, first meets Jesus. John tells us that the Jewish leaders did not enter the headquarters themselves in order to avoid becoming ritually impure and therefore unable to share in the Passover supper. According to Jewish law, anyone who entered this pagan area would be ritually unclean. John introduces a departure from the synoptic Gospels when he writes that the Jewish people have not yet celebrated the Passover. The synoptic Gospels describe the Last Supper as a Passover meal. In John's Gospel, the "Lamb of God" will be slain at the same time the lambs are slain for the ritual meal.

The exchange between Pilate and the Jewish leaders shows John's desire to lay the fault of Jesus' death at the feet of the Jewish leaders while striving to soften the involvement of the Roman government. This may be a reflection of the times in which John was writing rather than an actual portrayal of the events of the passion. At the time this gospel was written, the Jewish leaders were persecuting Christians in Jerusalem, while Christians were trying to show that a person could be Christian and a good Roman citizen at the same time. Unfortunately, many have misread this narrative throughout history and have unjustly persecuted the Jews as the ones directly responsible for Jesus' death.

Pilate asks what accusation the leaders bring against Jesus. The Jewish leaders interpret Pilate's words as doubting their condemnation of him, and they defend themselves, telling him that they would not have brought Jesus to him if he were not a criminal. When Pilate asks the Jewish leaders why they themselves did not put Jesus to death, he is indicating that he knows their true motives in handing Jesus over to him. They want him killed, but they do not want to carry the burden of being the ones who killed him. The author of the gospel views Roman crucifixion as the fulfillment of Jesus' words concerning his death, when Jesus spoke of being "lifted up." John presents this scene in two parts. In the first part, Pilate faces the leaders outside the headquarters; in the second part, Pilate faces Jesus inside this area. He goes back and forth between these two scenes.

Inside the headquarters, Pilate asks Jesus if he is the king of the Jews. This question, found in all the gospels, seems to be the real accusation brought against Jesus at the time of his passion. Jesus asks Pilate if this is his own question or if he has been prompted by others to ask it. Pilate answers that it is the Jewish people and leaders who have made the accusation. Jesus does not deny that he is a king, but he continues to speak in a spiritual vein as he has done throughout the gospel. His kingdom is a spiritual kingdom, not of this world. If he were from a worldly kingdom, he would have followers fighting to keep him from the hands of the Jewish leaders. Pilate views Jesus' words as an admission of his kingship, but Jesus does not directly accept the title and tells Pilate that he himself is the one using that title, not Jesus. The purpose behind Jesus' coming was to testify to the truth, that is, the presence of God in the world. Those committed to the truth are the ones who belong to God's kingdom and who truly hear Jesus' words of truth. Pilate asks a popular question of the philosophers of his time: "What is truth?"

Thereafter, Pilate goes outside to the Jewish leaders and claims that he has found no reason to condemn Jesus. To avoid any further confrontation over Jesus, he tries to employ the tradition of releasing a prisoner to them at Passover time. In John's Gospel, Pilate simply asks if they want him to free the "King of the Jews," and the crowd calls out for the freedom of Barabbas. John refers to him as a revolutionary. Pilate uses the term "King of the Jews" for Jesus to mock the Jewish leaders, for whom he has no love.

Lectio Divina

Spend 8 to 10 minutes in silent contemplation of the following passage:

Jesus' passion was an hour of darkness. In the midst of our own, the light of Christ still illumines our lives. Jesus, the king of creation, brings us salvation through his passion, death, resurrection, and ascension. We all experience dark moments, but Jesus urges us to remain faithful, as he did. In his darkest moment, Jesus is still the Light of the World.

✠ *What can I learn from this passage?*

Day 3: Preparation for the Crucifixion of Jesus (19:1–16)

A custom of the day was to have the accused, whether guilty or innocent, flogged before being crucified or released. Although Pilate finds no guilt in Jesus, he follows the custom of the day and has him scourged. Perhaps in an attempt to portray the Romans in a better light, John presents Pilate as working to free Jesus, although he gives no reason for this concern on the part of the procurator. Some commentators conjecture that Pilate did not wish to allow the Jewish leaders to have their way in putting Jesus to death.

The scourging has an ironic twist to it. The soldiers mock Jesus as a king, placing a crown of thorns on his head and a purple cloak on his shoulders. The author of the gospel and those who read his gospel with faith know that Jesus is truly the king of all nations, a spiritual king. The soldiers mockingly praise Jesus as the "King of the Jews."

After the scourging, Pilate apparently makes another attempt to free Jesus. He has him brought before the crowd, and he calls out, "Here is the man." The author and readers can recall that Jesus declared himself to be the Son of Man. Some commentators feel that John is alluding to this title in Pilate's words, and that the Roman ruler is unwittingly presenting the Son of Man to the world. Pilate states that he finds no guilt in Jesus, and that he refuses to have a hand in his death. The crowd cries out for the crucifixion of Jesus, and, in their call, they give the true reason for bringing Jesus before Pilate. Having earlier alleged that they had brought Jesus to Pilate because he claimed to be a king, they now declare that they want him crucified because he claims to be the Son of God. This identification of Jesus frightens Pilate.

Inside the praetorium again, Pilate asks Jesus, "Where are you from?" Jesus refuses to answer, and John offers no reason for Jesus' silence. Some commentators feel that Jesus' silence shows that Pilate would not have understood the meaning of Jesus' origin with the Father. When Pilate reminds Jesus that he has the power to release him or have him crucified, Jesus responds that all power comes from God. Since God has given a spiritual mission and power to the Jewish nation, Jesus claims that their sin is greater than that of Pilate. John, writing from the viewpoint of his own day, continues in his attempt to placate the Roman rulers by laying most of the blame on the Jewish leaders.

Pilate is anxious to release Jesus, but finally admits defeat when the people claim that Jesus is proclaiming himself to be a king and is thus making himself an enemy of Caesar. Pilate takes his seat on the stone platform for judgment, a place called Gabbatha in Hebrew. From this platform, Pilate taunts the Jewish leaders by presenting Jesus to them as their king and asking if he should crucify their king. Throughout the trial, Pilate unwittingly continues to proclaim the true identity of Jesus. The Jewish crowd responds that they have no king but Caesar. For the Jewish people the real king was God, and in proclaiming Caesar as their king, they sin against God. Jesus had warned earlier that anyone who rejected him would be rejecting the Father, and the author portrays this rejection as occurring at this time. Pilate hands Jesus over for crucifixion.

In this passage, John tells us that all of these events took place about noon on the preparation day for the Passover. This is another indication that John places the day of Jesus' death on the Passover feast, unlike the synoptic Gospels that place his death on the day after the Passover.

Lectio Divina

Spend 8 to 10 minutes in silent contemplation of the following passage:

God permits the power of darkness to dominate as Jesus stands before Pilate and states that Pilate would have no power over him if it were not given to him from above, that is, from God. Strange as it sounds, the good are often more powerful when they appear weak. Several years ago, a dying Sister of Saint Joseph gave a fitting example of the power of weakness. Bedridden and apparently useless in the eyes of many, she found a way to make her weakness valuable. When a nurse moved her to change her sheets, a bone would sometimes break. In the midst of such unbearable pain, she told her pastor who came to visit her, "God must have more for me to do." Offering up her suffering was a powerful prayer offered at the time of utmost weakness and pain. True followers of Jesus must never feel that their weakness is worthless.

✠ *What can I learn from this passage?*

Day 4: The Crucifixion of Jesus (19:17–30)

As the guards lead Jesus to his crucifixion, John tells us that Jesus carried his cross alone. Perhaps John did not know about the tradition that speaks of Simon of Cyrene helping Jesus carry his cross, or John may be stating that Jesus is responsible for his own destiny in obedience to the Father. He was crucified at a place called Golgotha in Greek, or "The Place of the Skull." The Latin word for Golgotha resembles the word Calvary, which is used often in English.

Pilate continues to taunt the religious leaders to the end by having the inscription "Jesus of Nazareth, the King of the Jews" placed on the cross. John alone tells of the Jewish leaders asking Pilate to remove this sign and to replace it with an inscription reading that he claimed to be the king of the Jews. The inscription placed on the cross usually told of the crime that led to crucifixion. Pilate declares, "What I have written, I have written." Jesus has come for all nations, and John alone tells us that the inscription was written in Latin, Greek, and Hebrew, the three common languages of his day, signifying that Jesus' message was for all nations.

The guards who brought the victim to crucifixion usually divided the garments of the crucified among them. Jesus, however, wore a seamless garment, and they decided to cast lots for his garment instead of tearing it. Some commentators have tried to determine if the seamless garment had some symbolic significance, but they disagree on its meaning. John tells us that the casting of lots for the garment fulfilled an Old Testament prophecy stating: "They divide my garments among them; for my clothing they cast lots" (Psalm 22:19).

John the Evangelist names the Mother of Jesus, Jesus' Mother's sister, Mary the wife of Clopas, and Mary Magdalene as the women standing below the cross. This is the only mention of Mary Magdalene thus far in the Gospel of John. She is named in the Gospel of Luke as the woman from whom seven devils were cast out (Luke 8:21). As Jesus looks upon his Mother, standing with the beloved disciple, he says, "Woman, here is your son," and, to the disciple, "Here is your mother." John tells us that the disciple took her into his care from that moment on. This passage has been interpreted as having a far deeper symbolic message. The beloved disciple represents all beloved disciples, that is, all the followers of Jesus, and the entire Church. Some commentators see Jesus as giving Mary the role of Mother of the Church.

The story about the Mother of Jesus links Jesus' passion with the gospel's opening story—the marriage feast at Cana. At that feast, Jesus called his mother by the title "Woman" and he claimed that his hour had not yet come. Now that his hour has arrived, Jesus addresses his mother with the same title of "Woman." The wedding feast at Cana, with its symbolic banquet and the water becoming wine, is seen by many commentators as an interpretation of Jesus' death and resurrection. The new life brought by Jesus is, like the new wine, better than the old.

Jesus cries out in thirst, and someone puts a sponge soaked in wine on a sprig of hyssop and offers it to him. It is most likely that a hyssop branch would not be strong enough to hold a sponge filled with wine, but its meaning may be a reference to the hyssop branch used to splash the blood of the lamb on the doorposts at the time of the first Passover (Exodus12:22). This would establish a link between Jesus' death as the new Lamb of God and the sacrifice of a lamb at the time of Passover. As

Jesus dies, he proclaims, "It is finished," and he gives up his spirit. Jesus, the earthly advocate, has finished his mission, and he now delivers up his spirit for all of creation.

Lectio Divina

Spend 8 to 10 minutes in silent contemplation of the following passage:

Mary appears at the beginning of the Gospel of John, and now she enters again at his crucifixion. Even in her grief over the horrible death being endured by Jesus, she is below the cross and prepared to accept a new role as the mother of all. As Jesus gave up his spirit, he left the world with an Advocate—the Holy Spirit; but he also left the world with Mary as the mother of all. After this, the Mother of Jesus would hold a high position in the life of the Church. In making Mary the spiritual mother of his disciples, he is making the disciples the children of his loving mother.

✠ *What can I learn from this passage?*

Day 5: The Burial of Jesus (19:31–42)

According to John's Gospel, the Passover and the Sabbath fell on the same day in the year Jesus was crucified. The Jewish leaders, desiring to have the bodies removed from the cross before the Sabbath, asked Pilate to have the legs of the crucified broken so that they would die sooner. With the legs broken, the crucified would suffocate because they could not lift up their bodies to catch a breath. After breaking the legs of the two thieves crucified on either side of Jesus, the guards decided not to break Jesus' legs because he was already dead. An eyewitness testified that a soldier pierced Jesus' side, and blood and water flowed forth. Many commentators, including many early interpreters of the Scriptures, saw in this flow of blood and water a symbol of the Eucharist and of Baptism. John tells us that the manner of Jesus' death fulfilled the Old Testament law concerning the lamb used for the Passover, namely, that none of the bones should be broken (Exodus 12:46). He also points to another Old Testament text from the prophet Zechariah that proclaimed that they looked upon "the one whom they have thrust through" (Zechariah 12:10).

John, in agreement with the synoptic Gospels, names Joseph of Arimathea as the one who buries Jesus, the sole gospel writer to mention that Joseph was a secret disciple of Jesus. Pilate grants Joseph permission to bury Jesus, and he and Nicodemus, the one who in an earlier episode debated with Jesus in the secrecy of night, prepare Jesus for burial. Nicodemus supplies the mixture of myrrh and aloes used at that time for burial purposes. According to John, the burial preparations of binding the body in cloth with perfumed oils were all performed. Because of the preparations for the Passover feast as well as the quickly approaching Sabbath, Joseph of Arimathea and Nicodemus bury Jesus in an unused tomb in a nearby garden.

Lectio Divina

Spend 8 to 10 minutes in silent contemplation of the following passage:

The dedication of some of Jesus' disciples does not end with his death. Two disciples, previously not known as disciples, come forward to bury Jesus' body. Like many followers of Jesus, they are willing to live with mystery. They do not understand how the one they thought to be the Christ could be killed, but they trust that this is not the end. Their example of courage and faith inspires us as present-day disciples of Jesus. Our call is to believe that Jesus is always present with us, even when we do not feel that presence.

✠ *What can I learn from this passage?*

Review Questions

1. What effect did Peter's denial of Christ have on Peter?
2. Why did Pilate attempt to save Jesus?
3. What did Jesus mean when he said that his kingdom was not of this world?
4. Why was it important for Jesus to be crucified outside of Jerusalem?
5. What didn't the guards tear Jesus' garments or break his legs? Explain.
6. What is the significance of blood and water flowing from the side of Jesus?
7. What happened at the burial of Jesus?

LESSON 8

The Resurrection of Jesus

JOHN 20:1—21:25

Then he (Jesus) said to Thomas, "Put your finger here and see my hands, and bring your hand and put it into my side, and do not be unbelieving, but believe." Thomas answered and said to him, "My Lord and my God" (John 20:27–28).

Opening Prayer (SEE PAGE 18)

Context

Part 1: John 20:1–31 Mary of Magdala finds the tomb empty and later sees two angels in white in the tomb. Jesus appears to her, announcing his ascension by saying that he is going to God the Father. He later appears to his disciples who are gathered together for fear of the religious leaders, and he bestows the Spirit upon them as he promised before he died. Jesus proves that he is truly raised from the dead to Thomas who wanted to touch Jesus' wounds, and expressed his belief by exclaiming: "My Lord and my God."

Part 2: John 21:1—21:25 Peter and six others go fishing and catch a large number of fish. When they recognize Jesus standing on the shore a short distance away, Peter dives in the water and swims to greet him. Jesus feeds them and asks Peter three times if he loves him. When Peter responds that he does, Jesus tells him to feed his lambs and tend to his sheep. The writer ends with the statement that Jesus' works could not fully be recorded because "if these were to be described individually, I do not think the whole world would contain the books that would be written" (21:25).

PART 1: GROUP STUDY (JOHN 20:1–31)

Read aloud John 20:1–31.

20:1–10 The empty tomb

John's description of the events surrounding the empty tomb differs slightly from those found in the synoptic Gospels. In these gospels, Mary Magdalene comes to the tomb with other women, but in John's Gospel, she arrives alone. The purpose of the visit in the synoptic Gospels was to finish the preparation of Jesus' body for a fitting burial, whereas John's Gospel has already revealed that Nicodemus took care of the preparation when he and Joseph of Arimathea buried Jesus immediately after his death. Mary Magdalene was apparently going to the tomb simply to visit the place of Jesus' burial.

When Mary discovers that the stone covering the burial place is set aside, she does not enter the tomb as reported in the synoptic Gospels, but she rushes off to tell Simon Peter and the disciple whom Jesus loved. Her immediate thought is that someone has stolen the body of Jesus. The beloved disciple reaches the tomb first, but out of deference to Peter he allows Peter to be the first to enter. The author of the gospel is apparently showing Peter's position of leadership. When the beloved disciple enters and sees the wrappings on the ground and the head covering rolled up by itself, he believes in the resurrection of Jesus. The author seems to be telling us that the presence and position of the burial coverings indicated that the body was not stolen. John reminds us that the disciples did not yet understand the message of the Hebrew Scriptures, which told that Jesus had to rise from the dead. The disciples return home.

20:11–18 The appearance of Mary of Magdala

Mary remains at the tomb, weeping. When she looks inside the tomb, she sees two angels in dazzling robes. The Gospel of John agrees with the number of angels found in Luke's portrayal of the empty tomb episode. When the angels ask her why she is weeping, Mary explains that the Lord has been taken away, and she does not know where they have placed his body. As she speaks with the angels, she turns, sees Jesus, and presumes he is the gardener. When Jesus asks her why she is weeping, she still does not recognize him. She begs him to tell her where he has laid the body, and if indeed he has taken it. When Jesus calls her by name, she recognizes him and addresses him with the Hebrew title Rabbouni, which means "teacher." This appearance of Jesus follows the usual resurrection encounter found in the gospels. Jesus appears and is at first not recognized, but then he speaks and is immediately known.

When Mary reaches out for Jesus, he tells her not to cling to him because he has not yet ascended to the Father. John could be giving us a message that the resurrection and the ascension of Jesus include the total mystery of Christ's glorification. Jesus does not return in his human form, but in the glorified form of one who now lives with God the Father in glory. Jesus instructs Mary to tell the disciples that he is ascending to God the Father. Jesus calls God "my Father and your Father, my God and your God." This may be a reference to his previous message that those who believe in the Son and are one with him also share in his glory with the Father.

Mary of Magdala rushes to the disciples and tells them all that has happened, reporting to them, "I have seen the Lord!"

20:19–31 Jesus appears to his disciples

On the evening of the first day of the week (Sunday), Jesus appears in the midst of the disciples, even though the doors of the place where they gathered were locked. John does not say that Jesus comes through the door as some artists have assumed, but that he appears in their midst. The disciples have gathered together, apparently in some secret place, fearing that the Jewish leaders will now come to have them killed as they did with Jesus. He addresses them with the customary greeting of "Peace." The significance of Jesus' greeting, however, has a far deeper meaning than any greeting in the past. He now brings with him the perfect harmony between his life and that of the Father. The disciples now share in the gifts of Christ's Resurrection.

Jesus shows the disciples the wounds in his hands and his side, thus confirming that the risen Lord is the same one who lived among them and was crucified. Jesus now bestows on his disciples their mission. The one who was sent by the Father now sends the disciples. He fulfills his promise by conferring the Holy Spirit on them, adding that those whose "sins you forgive are forgiven them, and whose sins you retain are retained." With the power of the Spirit comes the power of Christ to forgive sins.

Thomas, who arrives later, was not present when Jesus appeared, and he refuses to believe unless he can touch Jesus' wounds. A week later, apparently on another Sunday, Jesus comes and stands in their midst, despite the locked doors. Jesus invites Thomas, who is now present, to put his fingers into the wounds in his hands, and his hand into his side, and to become a believer. Thomas responds by giving the deepest affirmation of Jesus' person found in John's Gospel. Thomas calls Jesus ,"My Lord and my God!"

John's Gospel reaches out to those who have not lived with Christ, yet who have faith in him. Jesus declares that those people are blessed who have not seen but have believed in him. The author tells us that Jesus performed many more deeds in the presence of his disciples, but the words of this gospel were written that the reader may believe that Jesus is the Messiah, the Son of God, and "through this belief you may have life in his name." Most commentators believe that the original version of the gospel ended here.

Review Questions

1. What is significant about the story of the empty tomb?
2. Why did Jesus tell Mary of Magdala not to cling to him?
3. Why does Jesus breathe the Holy Spirit on the disciples? Explain.
4. How does Jesus' response to Thomas help us today?
5. Having completed our group study of the Gospel of John, overall how does this Gospel add to our understanding of Jesus? Discuss.

Closing Prayer (SEE PAGE 18)

Pray the closing prayer now or after *lectio divina*.

Lectio Divina (SEE PAGE 11)

Relax your body and maintain a posture of prayer (back straight, eyes shut, feet flat on the floor). This exercise can take as long as you want, but in the context of this Bible study, 10 to 20 minutes should be sufficient.

The meditations that follow are provided only to help group participants use this prayer form, but note that *lectio* is intended to bring one to a place of prayerful contemplation where the Word of God speaks to the hearer from his or her heart. See page 11 for further instruction.

The empty tomb (20:1–10)

The empty tomb points beyond itself to new life. A person once received an Easter card which had written on the front, "May you always find empty tombs in your life," and on the inside were the words, "and may you live a new life of resurrection as Jesus did." The card was saying that in the darkest moments of a person's life, the resurrected Christ will always be present to help us, because Jesus is not in the tomb. Rather, Jesus' mission continues in the world.

✠ *What can I learn from this passage?*

The appearance of Mary of Magdala (20:11–18)

Through his life, death, resurrection, and ascension, Jesus has joined heaven with earth. He experienced our human condition and in his exaltation, he carries that experience with him. He, as God, certainly could experience our human condition without becoming human, but for us, he fully entered our humanity. Through his life, he teaches us to live a life dedicated to love of God and neighbor. Through his death, he teaches us to trust the Lord as we abandon our lives into God's hands. Through his resurrection, he offers us hope for our own resurrection, inviting and encouraging us to live for eternal life with him. Through his exaltation, he links our humanity with his divinity and raises our humanity to a new and higher level.

✠ *What can I learn from this passage?*

Jesus appears to his disciples (20:19–31)

As Christians, we believe without seeing, and we are able to pray as Thomas did in the presence of Jesus: "My Lord and my God." Just as Jesus invited Thomas to touch his wounds, so he invites us to touch his wounds in the lives of people who are grieving, oppressed, rejected, or living in pain. Jesus not only invites us to touch his wounds in those who are suffering, but he calls us to heal these wounds in the best way we can. We may have doubts as Thomas did, but in the wounds of those around us we can experience the presence and compassion of the resurrected Christ and can cry out, "My Lord and my God."

✠ *What can I learn from this passage?*

PART 2: INDIVIDUAL STUDY (JOHN 21:1–25)

Day 1: The Appearance to the Seven Disciples (21:1–14)

This chapter, although found in all the early manuscripts of this gospel, is clearly an appendix added later, perhaps by a disciple of the author who shows some familiarity with the experiences and style of the original writer. The original gospel seems to end with the final verse of the previous chapter.

The gospel writer records six disciples who decide to follow Peter when he expresses his intent to go fishing. Among those who go fishing with this group are the sons of Zebedee. Although Zebedee's sons play an important role in the synoptic Gospels, this is the first mention of them in John's Gospel. Along with Zebedee's sons, Thomas, Nathanael, and two others, one of whom is the beloved disciple, comprise the group.

After fishing all night, the disciples catch nothing. At daybreak, Jesus calls to them from the shore, directing them to cast their nets off to the starboard side of the boat. As is usual in resurrection stories, they do not recognize Jesus at first. When they follow Jesus' directions, they catch so many fish that they cannot pull in the net. The beloved disciple, ever alert, is the first to recognize Jesus and says to Peter, "It is the Lord." In his excitement, Peter tucks in his garments, leaps into the sea, and swims to Jesus. Since the other disciples were not far from shore, they come to the shore in the boat. The disciples find that Jesus already has a fire ready, and, at his request, they bring him some fish. John mentions that they dragged in a net with one hundred fifty-three fish. This is most likely a number with some symbolic meaning, but commentators are unsure of what that meaning is. Despite the enormous catch of fish, the nets surprisingly were not torn.

John adds a human touch to his story as he has Jesus invite his disciples to come and eat breakfast. Jesus takes the bread and offers it to them, and he does the same with the fish; a eucharistic action. John indicates that no one asks Jesus who he is, because everyone knows his true identity.

The author adds that this is the third time Jesus appeared to his disciples after his resurrection. The people of Jesus' day believed that the number three had a special significance; the third appearance could indicate to the reader that Jesus had truly been raised from the dead.

Lectio Divina

Spend 8 to 10 minutes in silent contemplation of the following passage:

Jesus takes the initiative by calling out to his disciples and bidding them to come to him. At the shore, his invitation for them to enjoy breakfast shows that Jesus is still concerned with our human needs. He has been raised, but he really does not leave us to our daily needs without offering help. Just as Jesus, the Son of God, provides for our needs, so we must provide for the needs of others.

✠ *What can I learn from this passage?*

Day 2: Jesus and Peter (21:15–19)

After the meal, Jesus addresses Peter as Simon, asking him if he (Peter) loves him. When Peter answers that Jesus knows he loves him, Jesus tells him, "Feed my lambs." Jesus asks Peter this question a second time. When Peter answers the same way, Jesus tells him, "Tend my sheep." After asking the question a third time, Peter, hurt that the Lord should continually question him in this way, declares that Jesus knows all, and he certainly knows of his love. Jesus tells him, "Feed my sheep." These three declarations of love on the part of Peter offset Peter's three denials of Jesus at the time of the passion. Jesus gives Peter this opportunity to repent of his guilt. When Peter states that Jesus knows all, he is professing his belief that Jesus is God.

In an earlier chapter of the gospel, Jesus taught a lesson about the good shepherd who is willing to lay down his life for his sheep (10:11–18). When Peter professes his love for Christ, Jesus responds by making him the good shepherd of the sheep. Peter is not a hireling. Just as Jesus tended the sheep given him by God, so now Peter, the leader of the Twelve, is made the good shepherd. As a good shepherd, Peter will lay down his life for his sheep. Jesus tells him that he will no longer live for himself as he did in the past, but that he will be bound by others and carried away against his will. When Jesus has finished speaking, he says to Peter, "Follow me." At the time of the writing of this gospel, the author already knew the type of death Peter suffered at the hands of his persecutors.

Lectio Divina

Spend 8 to 10 minutes in silent contemplation of the following passage:

> In his rejection of Jesus, Peter gained knowledge of his own weakness and his need for Christ's support in living as one of his followers. He has been humbled by his rejection of Christ in the courtyard during the passion, but he has experienced forgiveness and a new form of dedication that would lead him to speak about his trust in Christ rather than in himself. As followers of Christ, we, like Peter, recognize our sinfulness and our need for support from Christ.

✠ *What can I learn from this passage?*

Day 3: The Beloved Disciple (21:20–25)

Peter asks Jesus about the beloved disciple who has been a central figure throughout the gospel. At this point, the author of this chapter identifies him as the one who rested against Jesus' chest during the Last Supper and asked Jesus to identify the betrayer. Jesus tells Peter to tend to his own business and not to concern himself about the beloved disciple. A rumor seems to have spread in the early Church that the beloved disciple was not to die until the Second Coming of Christ. Apparently the beloved disciple had already died at the time of this writing, and the author explains that Jesus never said he would not die. He simply gave an elusive answer to Peter's question, one which could have implied that the beloved disciple was to live until the Second Coming of Jesus. The author explains that Jesus never claimed that the disciple would live until he comes again.

Some commentators see a symbolic meaning to the title of "beloved disciple." Some disciples are called to leadership, such as Peter, but others, who are not called to this leadership, share in a special intimacy with Christ. Although the "beloved disciple" seems to refer to one of the disciples of Jesus, it could also refer to all beloved disciples to come. When Jesus is on the cross, he points to the beloved disciple and says to Mary, "Woman, behold your son," and he says to the beloved disciple, "Behold, your mother."

The Church views these words to Mary and the beloved disciple as a gesture that makes her the mother of all of Jesus' beloved disciples.

The author of this last chapter writes that he himself is a witness to the events written in the gospel. He is most likely a later witness who is repeating what he has heard preached within the community. He has heard much more that he could report, but like any true writer of the Scriptures, he had to make a choice about the material that would best present the message he wished to preach about Christ. Although this final author speaks as though he wrote the entire gospel, many commentators believe that he is responsible for this chapter alone.

Lectio Divina

Spend 8 to 10 minutes in silent contemplation of the following passage:

If we apply the idea that the beloved disciple includes all those who love Jesus and are certainly loved by Jesus, then we can interpret the scene to mean that beloved disciples would live on until the end of time. Jesus chose us, and this implies a call for us to become beloved disciples of a loving Jesus. The foundation of Jesus' life and message is God's love for us and our love for God and for all people.

✠ *What can I learn from this passage?*

Review Questions

1. Why was the miraculous catch of fish so important in recognizing Jesus?

2. Why did Jesus ask Peter three times if Peter loved him? Explain.

3. Since Jesus said the beloved disciples would remain until he comes, is it possible that the beloved disciples are still alive today? In what way are you Christ's beloved disciple? Reflect on God's love for you.

4. What makes some commentators think that John did not write the last chapter of the gospel?

About the Author

William A. Anderson, DMin, PhD, is a presbyter of the diocese of Wheeling-Charleston, West Virginia. Director of retreats and parish missions, professor, catechist, spiritual director, and former pastor, he has written extensively on pastoral, spiritual, and religious subjects. Father Anderson earned his doctor of ministry degree from St. Mary's Seminary & University in Baltimore and his doctorate in sacred theology from Duquesne University in Pittsburgh.

ALSO AVAILABLE IN THE
LIGUORI CATHOLIC BIBLE STUDY SERIES

Introduction to the Bible:
Overview, Historical Context, and Cultural Perspectives
ISBN 978-0-7648-2119-6 • 112 pages

Words of Praise for
INTRODUCTION TO THE BIBLE

"This very useful catechetical work, *Introduction to the Bible*, provides an excellent and very accessible introduction to the study of sacred Scripture. With the explanation and introduction to *lectio divina*, the reader will discover praying the Scriptures as an important spiritual practice. I am certain this text will be very useful to young people and adults who wish to learn about sacred Scripture, the history of salvation it makes known to us, and the cultural and historical context of its many books."

MOST REVEREND MICHAEL J. BRANSFIELD,
BISHOP OF WHEELING-CHARLESTON

The Gospel of Matthew: Proclaiming the Ministry of Jesus
ISBN 978-0-7648-2120-2 • 160 pages

The Gospel of Mark: Revealing the Mystery of Jesus
ISBN 978-0-7648-2121-9 • 144 pages

The Gospel of Luke: Salvation for All Humanity
ISBN 978-0-7648-2122-6 • 144 pages

For more information,
call 800-325-9521 or visit liguori.org

CPSIA information can be obtained at www.ICGtesting.com
Printed in the USA
LVOW06s1912130414

381441LV00005BA/6/P